Rainbows
of
Intelligence

Rainbows
of
Intelligence

Exploring How Students Learn

Sue Teele

Foreword by Thomas Armstrong,
author of "Multiple Intelligences in the Classroom"

Skyhorse Publishing

First Skyhorse Publishing edition 2015.

Skyhorse Publishing books may be purchased in bulk at special discounts for sales promotion, corporate gifts, fund-raising, or educational purposes. Special editions can also be created to specifications. For details, contact the Special Sales Department, Skyhorse Publishing, 307 West 36th Street, 11th Floor, New York, NY 10018 or info@skyhorsepublishing.com.

Skyhorse® and Skyhorse Publishing® are registered trademarks of Skyhorse Publishing, Inc.®, a Delaware corporation.

Visit our website at www.skyhorsepublishing.com.

10 9 8 7 6 5 4 3 2 1

Library of Congress Cataloging-in-Publication Data is available on file.

Cover design by Tracy E. Miller

Print ISBN: 978-1-63220-565-0
Ebook ISBN: 978-1-63220-981-8

Printed in the United States of America

Contents

Foreword

The rainbow is a powerful metaphor for learning and growth. Cross-culturally it symbolizes transformation, the meeting of heaven and earth, the link between the divine and the earthly, and the bridge from one stage of learning to another. In this book, Sue Teele uses it to shed light on the topic of multiple intelligences. Dr. Teele helps educators who are working with multiple intelligences reconcile what appears to be a contradiction within MI theory: How can there be seven distinct intelligences, and yet at the same time, an almost infinite variety of ways that people show their smarts? By using the spectrum of colors to illustrate her point, Teele introduces us to the basic palate of colors we all learned in kindergarten, and shows us how we can combine these colors (translated into seven distinct intelligences) to create a great diversity of hues (an infinite variety of intelligences). Hence, each student, and each curriculum strategy used in the classroom potentially represents a unique blend of the seven primary colors-intelligences.

Rainbows of Intelligence: Exploring How Students Learn provides a wealth of ideas, strategies, resources, and reflections on how to use multiple intelligences to help each student express his or her own personal learning rainbow. Sue's personal and engaging style of writing combines her own experiences as an educational researcher, teacher, and grandparent, with some of the latest findings in the field of brain research, cognitive psychology, and human development, to create a work that many teachers will find refreshing and useful to their work in integrating multiple intelligences into the curriculum.

Sue's comments on the need for movement in learning, the importance of going beyond "phonics" in learning to read, and the joy of exploring the richness of connections between math and music, for example, are reflections that badly need to be heard in today's test-driven school system. Her own MI inventory, the *Teele Inventory of Multiple Intelligences (TIMI)*, speaks volumes in its statistical findings that students identify less and less with linguistic and logical-mathematical images of learning, the more they stay in school. This should send a message to policy makers that the answer to the problem of education today does not lie in piling on the textbook and math problems! Instead, Sue invites us into a world of possibilities with her engaging lesson plans that span the spectrum of multiculturalism, ecology, the life cycle, optics, and many other fascinating subjects.

Truly, this book itself serves as a rainbow, taking readers from the land of theory to the world of practice, in one gliding ride that teachers will find gives them joy and more flexibility in practicing their very important art of education.

THOMAS ARMSTRONG

Preface

The ideas for this book have been evolving over the past four years as I have continued to study, research, and apply Howard Gardner's theory of multiple intelligences in different educational environments. I have continued the collaboration in my research with two special friends, Jo Gusman and Thomas Armstrong, and I value and respect their talents and expertise. My correspondence over the past four years with Howard Gardner has challenged me to concentrate on discovering ways the educational community can provide greater opportunities for all students to succeed.

I recently had the pleasure of teaching for a week at the new Dream Planet International School in Okinawa, Japan. That experience has deeply influenced my commitment to work diligently in an effort to redesign the educational system to more effectively acknowledge the unique gifts and talents of all individuals. While I was teaching, I witnessed teachers at the school discover and develop their own unique abilities to teach.

The new spatial model I am presenting in this book is designed to build upon multiple intelligences and address the complex pathways that individuals use to process information. The analogy with the rainbows, spectrum, prisms, and colors is very appropriate. When students are provided the opportunity to let their "lights shine," they can reveal a full prism of abilities that might never be discovered if they are not allowed to use their full spectrum of intelligences.

I am deeply concerned that in the concentrated effort to improve academic achievement and raise the level of standards for student success, we have ignored the most important ingredient for success, the focus on the uniqueness of each student's ability to learn. This book is written in an effort to emphasize the need to explore how students learn and to consider that domain during all the discussions of academic standards and methods for assessing students.

Many individuals have assisted me in creating this book. First, I want to thank my family, who have supported me during the research and writing. My husband, Steve, has been my number one supporter, and I am very grateful that he has always believed in my abilities. My two sons, Brett and Chris, have been very much a part of my motivation to improve the quality of education and both have been instrumental in my being able to develop my ideas for the future. My two daughters-in-law have immediately been brought into the multiple intelligences world and have contributed in many ways to this book. My seven grandchildren have provided a living laboratory for me to study how children develop in their progressions of learning. My mom has always been interested in learning about my research and what makes her dendrites continue to branch. My staff at the University of California, Riverside, has assisted me in creating some of the ideas in this book.

I began to think about this book 2 years ago and it seems that every opportunity I have been given has had a direct influence on the evolution of this book. Part I was designed to present current research findings and establish a rationale for the spatial model I have presented. The units in Part II will demonstrate for teachers how to develop lessons that integrate the intelligences, offer multiple measures of assessment, and provide methods for incorporating content standards into each lesson.

This book was created to acknowledge that all individuals have their own unique rainbows of intelligence and, given the proper opportunities to shine, they will demonstrate academic achievement by applying their full spectrum of human potential. We must work together to ensure that all students are given the opportunity to achieve success.

SUE TEELE, PhD

About the Author

S ue Teele, PhD, is the author of several books, including *The Multiple Intelligences School: A Place for All Students to Succeed*, and a spatial inventory, *The Teele Inventory for Multiple Intelligences*. She is the Director of Education Extension at the University of California, Riverside, where she administers over 20 different programs for 8,000 to 10,000 educators a year. She created the first and only certificate in the study of multiple intelligences in the world. She is also the director of the Renaissance Project, a research study that examines the theory of multiple intelligences and its impact in the educational setting. Dr. Teele is a member of the Committee on Accreditation for the California Commission on Teacher Credentialing.

Dr. Teele has given numerous inservices, courses, and keynote addresses to elementary and secondary schools, colleges, and businesses throughout the United States and internationally. She consults with schools and districts that are interested in implementing the theory of multiple intelligences into their educational environment. Her focus is always on exploring ways to assist all students to reach their full potential.

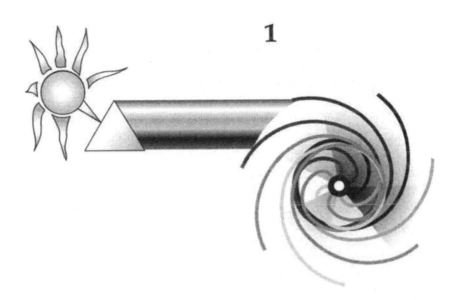

1

A Focus on How Students Learn

Introduction

It has been stated that all students can learn and succeed, but not in the same way and not on the same day. What does this mean for today's educational environments? We are in a dramatic paradigm shift to incorporating standards and accountability for all students in the basic skills areas. In this endeavor to achieve higher academic standards and student success, we seem to have forgotten an important piece for solving the academic puzzle. That piece is the focus on how students learn and the relationship of intelligence to the learning process.

Throughout the 20th century, psychologists have studied the nature of human intelligence as a way to predict school performance. They have examined different approaches to or interpretations of intelligence. Most psychologists agree that individuals are unique and differ in their ability to understand abstract ideas, to reason in critical and creative ways, to adapt effectively to environmental situations, and to apply information from one experience to another. Intellectual performances may vary on different days and in different ways when measured by a variety of criteria. Individuals appear to process with their own rainbows of intelligence; no two individuals process in the same way.

I have always been fascinated by the beauty a rainbow provides at the end of a rainstorm. Recently I was driving from Monterey to Modesto, California, and had to travel through an area known as Deadman's Pass. As I began to drive into the pass, a blinding rainstorm started. It was raining so hard that I could barely see the road. I felt a sudden sense of fear because I knew the deadly reputation of the road. I proceeded slowly. The rain was pelting my windshield so intensely that I debated whether I should pull over to the side of the road. Suddenly, I saw a rainbow right in front of me. The rainbow was positioned in a way that indicated the direction I should follow. In the next two hours, I witnessed several more rainbows. They seemed to be providing a colorful path for me to follow. I have never experienced so many rainbows during such a short time period. I have begun to look at rainbows from a different perspective—one of providing a sense of hope, direction, and guiding light.

That experience provided the vision for this book. I began to research rainbows and discovered a relationship between rainbows, colors, and the theory of multiple intelligences. I realized that I was embarking on creating a different way to examine the theory of multiple intelligences. When Howard Gardner, the originator of the theory of multiple intelligences, introduced the naturalist intelligence as the eighth intelligence several years ago, I struggled with the placement of this additional intelligence because it did not seem to fit with the other seven. The characteristics of this intelligence seemed to overlap characteristics of several other intelligences. I attempted to draw pictures for the *Teele Inventory for Multiple Intelligences* (1992), an inventory created to help to identify how individuals process information using the multiple intelligences. I found I had great difficulty creating specific drawings for the naturalist intelligence because of the overlap. I realized I was comfortable with the seven primary intelligences remaining as they had been defined. I had to design a way to explain the naturalist intelligence and any other intelligence that might be introduced in the future.

When I witnessed the rainbows, a new idea started to evolve, focusing on the colors of the rainbow and the primary, secondary, and complementary colors of the color wheel. I recognized the need to refocus thinking more on the uniqueness of each student's ability to learn.

In the first six chapters of this book, I present several views of the nature of intelligence and discuss how the educational community must achieve a more balanced approach to teaching and learning. Chapter 1 explores different approaches to understanding intelligence. Chapter 2 examines some aspects of brain research and its relationship to student learning. Chapter 3 takes a second look at the theory of multiple intelligences and its applications and implications for the classroom. Chapter 4 examines ways to effectively prepare students for the 21st century and updates gender research in reference to multiple intelligences. Chapter 5 introduces the rainbows of intelligence model, which presents a different approach to examining multiple intelligences. Chapter 6 provides suggestions for changing educational environments to reflect more effectively how students learn.

Chapter 7 presents units I developed that revolve around the idea of colors. These units can be adapted for any grade level and content area.

As I began my research for this book, I realized I needed to better understand the nature of intelligence and where the strong educational movement toward standardization and objective testing fits within the construct of intelligence.

Several different approaches to intelligence have been identified. It is important to have a brief understanding of these approaches to gain a broader perspective of what it means to provide effective learning environments for all students. The four different approaches are the psychometric approach, developmental progressions, the psychobiological approach, and multiple forms of intelligence.

Psychometric Approach

The psychometric approach acknowledges a single, unitary, quantitative concept of intelligence. Binet's test (Binet & Simon,

1916) measured motor development, cognitive abilities, memory tests, and divergent-productive thinking abilities and introduced a single score for measurement. His concept of mental age and chronological age has been a foundation for intelligence evaluation. That same year the Stanford-Binet scale was developed. This scale also measured intelligence as a single trait. The test reported national norms and was used to measure abstract thinking. The Wechsler scales, introduced in the 1940s, was the first test to give the Stanford-Binet scale any competition. Wechsler began to recognize the multiple aspects of intelligence. His test had two categories, verbal and performance, and contributed to the intellectual evaluation of individuals from preschool age to adults. Spearman (1927) argued that all intellectual performances drew upon a single, underlying general intellectual or "g" factor. Spearman introduced the first and simplest possible factor model, which meant that any test in the intellectual category had only one common factor, "g," as well as a unique specific factor, "s." There has not been complete agreement on how "g" should be defined.

> *The psychometric approach focuses only on two ways to learn: linguistic and logical-mathematical.*

The psychometric approach focuses primarily on two ways to learn: linguistic and logical-mathematical. It is easy to quantify, is measurable, and can be compared in a standardized way. The current movement in education in the United States leans strongly toward a psychometric approach because it can be used to compare one student to another or one school or district to another. It is important to utilize the psychometric approach in education as one of several ways to assess students. However, there is a danger if this approach becomes the single means to measure student achievement, because it demonstrates only one or two ways students learn. Students' minds are multifaceted instruments that cannot be completely defined through any one type of assessment. Assessment should include not only standardized and criterion-referenced tests, but also performance, problem, product-based, and portfolio assessment to accurately assess the multiple ways students learn.

Developmental Progressions

A second approach to intelligence is developmental progressions. Piaget (1972) offered a developmentally based concept of intelligence and discussed how individuals develop progressively at different ages and continually shift between assimilation of new information into their existing cognitive structures and accommodation of those structures to new information. He stated that the key to understanding intelligence and the operation of the human mind is perceiving how humans acquire and use knowledge. Piaget found that children transition through a number of very different stages of development: from the sensorimotor stage of infancy to the preoperational, intuitive stage of early childhood, onto the concrete, operational stage of middle childhood, and finally to the formal operational stage of adolescence. Piaget believed that normal children pass through different stages of development at specific ages.

I decided to test parts of Piaget's theory on a 6-year-old boy, whom I shall call Shawn, to explore if there were definite stages of processing or if these stages differed in the same individual when given different tasks. Shawn was born 2 months prematurely and experienced serious hemorrhaging in his brain soon after birth. Even with his complications at birth, by 6 I found him to possess strong intellectual ability. He was able to read stories, understand place value, and verbally count numbers up to 2,000,000 before he entered kindergarten. I asked him to do several activities to explore how he learned. The first activity was with pennies and addressed the question of sameness or difference. He was shown two rows of six pennies each and asked to identify if the rows were the same or different. For the first two rows, he stated they were the same. He was then shown a second two rows. The second two rows looked like the following:

He experienced no difficulty seeing the similarities and differences between the two rows. He demonstrated intuitive correspondence by making an immediate optical spatial correspondence with the two rows of coins and was able to make equivalence even when the coins were displaced. He saw the one-to-one correspondence between the two rows without counting the coins and was able to use concrete, operational processing ability.

According to Piaget (1951, 1972), Shawn was beginning to understand the construction of numbers and master the operation of coordinating the differences and progressive reversibility of thought. His intuitive spatial ability allowed him to determine the elements of the corresponding rows. He could grasp the idea of equal units and the fact that they differed one from the other by their relative order of enumeration. This ability was beyond his developmental age.

Piaget believed there were three developmental stages through which children progress in understanding the notion of random mixture and irreversibility. The first, from 4 to 7 years, is a mixture of total displacement of elements, which creates a state of disorder that results in the return of the elements to their original order and the inability to grasp the random nature of mixture. The second, from 7 to 11 years, is when the child can construct and intuitively perceive change and permutation, combinations and reversibility, and the interrelatedness of operations. The third, from 11 to 12 years, is when the child is able to understand the process of random mixture and see an operative system of permutation.

In a second activity, Shawn was given a box containing 10 marbles, 5 blue ones and 5 white ones, and asked to predict what would happen to them when they were tilted. In spite of different variations each time, he seemed to expect a simple return of the marbles to their original places. He saw mixture at first, but could not perceive the idea of permutation or change of order. He had been able to recognize the same operations of placement or order with the coins in the first exercise, but could not make the transformation to the marbles. He could not go beyond the first stage to understand permutation and combinations of reversibility of operations with the marbles, but he could with the coins.

Leinhardt (1988) provided four different classes of students' mathematical knowledge: intuitive, concrete, computational, and

---

> **Each individual is unique in
> each of his or her processing skills.**

---

conceptual. I discovered in this young boy that, when given some activities to perform, he could move from intuitive to concrete to computational knowledge and even began to demonstrate that he was beginning to understand conceptual knowledge; yet, in some activities, he could not.

My work with Shawn made me realize that each individual is unique in each of his or her processing skills. A child will be more advanced in some skills than others based on the combinations of skills he or she uses to accomplish a given task. We cannot assume that because a child is capable when given one task, he or she will be able to transfer that skill to another task or is developmentally strong in similar tasks. I suggest that children's developmental progressions of ability differ individually and depend on the unique combinations of the ways they process information and the different tasks they are given. Perhaps all the recent work conducted on the interrelatedness of the brain should be considered as we explore the developmental progressions of each individual.

*Children's developmental progressions of
ability differ individually and depend on the
unique combinations of the ways they process
information and the different tasks they are given.*

Vygotsky (1978) suggested that all intellectual abilities are social in origin and operate in zones of proximal development; the distance between the level of problem solving that can be accomplished by someone working independently and the level that can be accomplished with some assistance from others. Teachers become both instructors and facilitators of the learning process, and must know when to assist students and when to allow them to learn independently. The role of the teacher is to move back and forth continuously from teacher to facilitator who can encourage independent thought.

*Teachers must consider the
students' zones of proximal development
and move from teacher to facilitator.*

Vygotsky said that intelligence is a function of activity that is mediated through material and psychological tools and contact with other human beings. He stated that during infancy, the child's primary activity is emotional contact. At age 2, the manipulation of objects becomes important. From ages 3 to 7, role play and symbolic activity emerge. From ages 7 to 11, an emphasis on formal study in school develops. During adolescence, the blending of interpersonal relations and exploration of careers begins.

Vygotsky				
0–2 years Emotional contact	2 years Manipulation of objects	3–7 years Role play and symbolic activity	7–11 years Emphasis on formal study in school	12–18 years Blending of interpersonal relations and exploration of careers

In the past 3 years, we have been fortunate to add two daughters-in-law and seven grandchildren to our family. This has provided me first hand opportunities to study the developmental progressions of children from newborn to 14 years of age. I have observed my two young granddaughters, a 1-year-old, and a 2-year-old, and have noted their differences. The infant, Angie, wants to be held and to maintain emotional contact with a member of the family. The toddler, Chrissy, is constantly moving, touching objects, and exploring her world. She wants to be in the same room with her older brothers and sisters, and will often imitate their actions, such as coloring or playing with toys. She enjoys manipulating objects such as cups and blocks, and can fit different shapes into their corresponding openings on a ball. She also enjoys music and books that have musical sounds.

My other five grandchildren are 5, 6, 10, 11, and 14 years old. Davey, who is 5 and just began kindergarten, enjoys working with puzzles and playing with cars and trucks. He creates symbolic places with his cars and trucks. He has begun to show interest in learning about shapes, colors, letters of the alphabet, and counting. Candace, the 6-year-old, has become interested in counting, learning new words, reading, writing, spelling, and performing mathematical functions. Her positive kindergarten experience has made her an eager learner with a great desire to read and write. I am convinced that the kindergarten experience must be a positive introduction to the learning process and must establish a foundation for introduction to formal study.

Tony, who is 10 years old, is serious about his studies in school and is capable of processing complex information. I recently worked with him as part of a keynote presentation at a multiple intelligences conference. I wanted him to understand the three parts of the brain and how the brain functions. I also asked him to explain to the audience the differences in developmental progressions between his younger brother and three sisters. Much to the amazement of the audience, he was able to discuss what each child could and could not do and had an excellent grasp of their capabilities and their developmental progressions.

My other two grandchildren, Brian and Kristin, exhibit special gifts in different intelligences. Brian, who is 11, is very musically talented and quite bodily-kinesthetic. He is an excellent soccer player and loves working with spatial games on the computer. He has begun to place more emphasis on formal study in school. Kristin, who is 14, is a strong academic student who is very linguistic and interpersonal. She is exploring careers and is considering broadcasting. She has demonstrated her maturity in that area by acting and giving speeches at school.

> *Different teaching methods are*
> *required to encourage students to learn from their*
> *dominant ways of processing and to build on*
> *previous successful experiences.*

Feuerstein (1981) said that intelligence results from experience and that our cognitive ability can be modified. His theory of structural cognitive modifiability states that learning can be transformed to enable one to learn better. New learning experiences are built on past successes and there is a progression between the two. The schooling experience can modify and enhance how individuals learn by providing alternative educational strategies that enable one's potential to be maximized. This is an important aspect of the theory of multiple intelligences. Different teaching methods are required to encourage students to learn from their dominant ways of processing and to build on previous successful experiences.

Psychobiological Approach

Several researchers have studied the brain from a biological perspective to explore new ideas about what intelligence is and how to measure it (Ceci, 1990; Reed and Jensen, 1993; Sylwester, 1995). Ceci's bioecological theory of intelligence argues that no one cognitive potential or "g" factor exists. Instead, there are multiple potentials. He states that knowledge and aptitude are inseparable and that environmental, biological, metacognitive, and motivational variables are all found within the context of intelligence. These connections will be actively explored in the next few years.

A psychobiological perspective of intelligence strongly supports a multifaceted view of intelligence, rather than a single-factor theory. It incorporates awareness of gender differences in some cognitive activities. Cognitive functions occur in multiple, specific areas of the brain and are influenced by a combination of genetics, personal life experiences, and situations.

LeDoux (1996) and Goleman (1995) emphasized the important role that emotions play in learning. They discussed how the emotional centers and the cognitive centers of the brain constantly interact and interplay.

The emotional centers of the brain can impede the academic success of the prefrontal cognitive part of the brain. The brain remains flexible and evolves throughout an individual's life. It is altered based on life experiences, situations, and circumstances.

Multiple Forms of Intelligence

If no two individuals process information in exactly the same way, can we continue to ignore this fact and support only a psychometric approach to intelligence? Substantial research supports the fact that individuals process in multiple, interactive, and complex ways. This leads directly to the fourth approach, multiple forms of intelligence.

Sternberg at Yale University and Gardner at Harvard University are proponents of the concept of multiple forms of intelligence. Sternberg (1985) proposed a triarchic theory of successful intelligence comprising fundamental aspects of intelligence—analytical, creative, and practical. He indicated that successful intelligence involves using intelligence to achieve goals. He encouraged a balance between these three aspects of intelligence. He stated that only the first aspect, analytical, can be measured by standardized tests (the psychometric approach to intelligence). Sternberg found that practical intelligence is highly valued in the workplace because it enables individuals to perceive subtle messages people send to one another and to understand the more practical aspects of life. Along with Elena Grigorenko, he examined the complexity of studying cognitive abilities in different cultures and found differences in how cultures define and reward intelligence.

STERNBERG'S TRIARCHIC THEORY

- *Analytical*
- *Creative*
- *Practical*

Gardner (1983) proposed the theory of multiple intelligences, which consists of seven different ways to process information: linguistic, logical-mathematical, spatial, musical, bodily-kinesthetic, intrapersonal, and interpersonal.

Sternberg's (1985, 1988) triarchic theory and Gardner's (1983, 1993) multiple intelligences theory go beyond the traditional definition of intelligence. These two theories focus on individual differences among students. They try to match each student's ability profile to a variety of different educational methods rather than teaching in only one way and expecting all students to be able to understand that method.

There continue to be remarkable discoveries in brain research and in how individuals learn. Chapter 2 highlights some of these discoveries. These discoveries will influence both our educational system and our future workforce. We must examine ways to redesign our educational system to allow all students to develop their intellectual abilities to full potential.

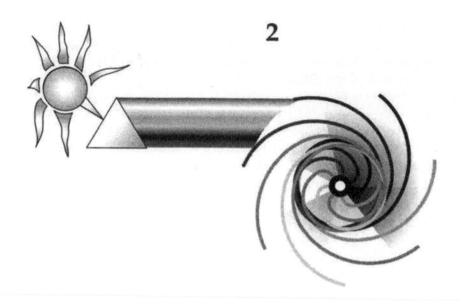

2

Recent Research on the Brain

As we examine the relationship between the theory of multiple intelligences and the changes we should make in education, I offer a new model that builds on this theory and considers the complex pathways that individuals utilize to process information. We need to understand the working relationship between the brain and the uniqueness of each student's ability to learn.

We each learn in a highly personal, individual way; we add and sort out new information, and revise all the previously acquired information. No two individuals have the same profile of intelligences or process information in the same manner.

> *We each learn in a highly personal,*
> *individual way. No two individuals have*
> *the same profile of intelligences.*

Hart (1983) stated that the brain is the core and the storehouse of personal existence. We need to think of intelligence as a process that incorporates the entire brain. The brain is not simply right or left hemispheres, but a whole entity with constant interaction between both sides. We can define our intelligence as the capacity to carry out a multitude of tasks that range from breathing, crying, registering pain, seeing, and hearing, to making highly complex decisions.

The Human Brain

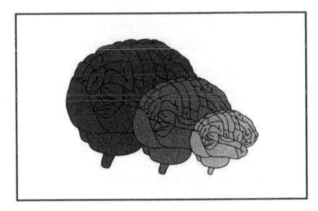

The human brain is a multimodal apparatus, which weighs about 3 pounds and contains more than 90% of the body's neurons. The brain of a 6-month-old baby is about one-half the size of an adult brain. The brain of a 3-year-old child is about three-fourths the size of an adult brain. The brain of a 5-year-old is about nine-tenths its potential size (Jensen, 1995; Sylwester, 1995).

Brain Sizes

6 months	3 years	5 years
1/2	3/4	9/10

The brain operates as an intricate, interconnected system. Recent findings suggest that the brain's organization can be viewed in a modular way, rather than in a hierarchial sense of organization (Sylwester, 1995). The brain regulates many body systems such as breathing, pumping blood, and digesting food. Language and use of symbols are functions of the brain. Among mammals, humans have the largest brain in comparison to body size (Simon, 1997).

The brain works through a constantly changing interaction of the brainstem, the limbic system, and the cerebral cortex. The brain stem is located at the top of the spinal column and is about 3 inches long and the size of a thumb. This part is the oldest and

---

THE BRAIN

- **Brain stem**
- **Limbic system**
- **Cerebral cortex**

---

smallest part of the brain and it operates many systems of the body that are essential to life. The brainstem regulates respiration, heart rate, blood pressure, and digestion. It makes automatic decisions that keep individuals alive (Simon, 1997). All sensorimotor information flows through the brainstem.

The cerebellum is at the lower back of the brain and controls automatic movements. The limbic system is folded around the brainstem and is the connection to the cerebral cortex. It is the brain's center for regulating emotions. Through the amygdala, the structure that controls emotional processing, the limbic system filters and processes sensory information. The hippocampus classifies and stores information. The thalamus and hypothalamus are the structures in the limbic system that assist in regulating emotional life and physical safety (Sylwester, 1995). The limbic system acts as a gatekeeper for the different parts of the brain and controls the relationship between emotions and learning. This system is being recognized as very important because of recent research on the relationship of emotions to operations of the brain (Goleman, 1995; LeDoux, 1996).

The cerebral cortex is the newest and by far the largest part of the brain. The cellular part of the cortex is called the gray matter.

Beneath the gray matter is the white matter, which makes up most of this part of the brain (Mathers, 1992). All the learning achieved in formal education occurs in the cerebral cortex. Language, symbols, and abstract thinking reside in this part of the brain. The cortex is composed of two cerebral hemispheres, which are largely mirror images. If we examine these two hemispheres, we see that each side has different functions that enable individuals to utilize all of the different multiple intelligences. The hemispheres are linked together by the corpus callosum, which is a thick bundle of nerves. The functions of the two hemispheres are examined in the following table.

The Two Hemispheres of the Brain

Left Hemisphere	Right Hemisphere
Right hand touch & movement	Left hand touch & movement
Speech	Spatial construction
Language and writing	Face recognition
Linear thinking	Music processing
Analysis	Nonverbal matters

The left cerebral hemisphere in most people processes speech, language, and sequential, logical, rational, and analytical content. The right cerebral hemisphere is thought to be less critical and more creative. It provides the ability to process music, patterns, shapes, and forms. It handles spatial, musical, nonverbal, and intuitive matters. Although the two hemispheres perform different tasks, they collaborate through the corpus callosum on most tasks.

Both hemispheres work in collaboration. Some gifted individuals, such as Leonardo da Vinci and Albert Einstein, may have been able to connect several areas of their brains together, which allowed them to see new visions and to solve problems no one had accomplished before. Einstein (Cwiklik, 1987) formulated the theory of relativity and was also an excellent violinist. He was a scientist who saw beauty and symmetry in the world around him. Da Vinci was both a great artist and a great scientist.

I have found that when I use a shelled walnut to show what the brain looks like, individuals can visualize the two hemispheres of the brain when they can actually see a representation of it. The center of the walnut depicts the corpus callosum, the connection between the two hemispheres.

Recent studies have revealed that the brain's cortex comprises 85% of the mass of the human brain. According to Sylwester (1995), the brain consists of tens of billions of cortical neurons that regulate cognitive thinking activities and even more glial cells that support and feed the neurons. Neurons come in many sizes and shapes. A bundle of neurons is called a nerve (Simon, 1997).

Neurons look like trees and have branches that are called dendrites. Dendrites are tubular extensions that receive and carry messages to and from other neurons and will grow when stimulated.

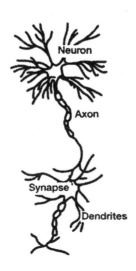

As the brain builds more branches, more connections can be made. When dendrites branch, abstract thinking increases. As the dendrites spread, they allow individuals to think more clearly and in more complex ways. The dendrites carry electrical signals to other neurons. Neurons pass messages through long fibers called axons. Axons extend the electrical signals and travel through the body (Mathers, 1992). Axons look like caterpillars as they extend to other neurons. Messages are carried across small openings called synapses. Glial cells are like glue and they form protective layers around nerve fibers.

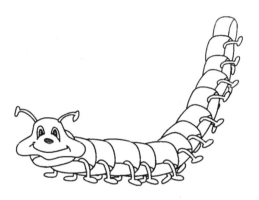

Thinking is a dynamic process. If the brain is not used, the dendrites do not branch out. Conversely, more dendrites or branches can grow on the brain when it is stimulated.

The cortex is six layers thick and the cortical neurons are arranged in minicolumns of 100 neurons that run vertically through the six layers of the cortex (Sylwester, 1995). Each column processes very specific tasks. One hundred of these columns are combined into magnocolumns, which each have over 10,000 neurons. These magnocolumns integrate the more complex parts of different tasks that require the involvement of more than one minicolumn at a time.

The corpus callosum provides pathways for continuous exchanges between the two hemispheres. These pathways allow two to three different intelligences to operate simultaneously from both sides of the brain.

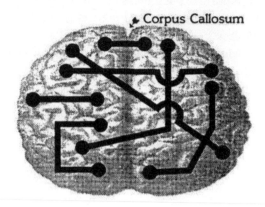

The cerebral cortex is divided into two hemispheres and each hemisphere is divided into four lobes: temporal, parietal, occipital, and frontal. Using positron emission tomography and functional magnetic resonance imaging, researchers have monitored regional brain activity in normal subjects and have identified specific regions of the cerebral cortex that are activated during certain cognitive tasks.

Much research has been directed toward understanding visual perception and language tasks. Recently researchers (National Institutes of Health, 1996) have begun to compile anatomical and functional data into a single electronic map of the human cerebral cortex. Linguistic, logical-mathematical, spatial, musical, and bodily-kinesthetic intelligences are currently being studied in the brain, and analyzed as the manner in which each operates individually and in connection with the other intelligences.

The temporal lobe is located above and behind the ears. It is the area that processes hearing and speech. Understanding language, auditory processing and perception, and nonspeech auditory perception such as music all take place in this lobe.

The parietal lobe is located at the top of the head. It responds to sensations of touch and motor control. It combines sensory

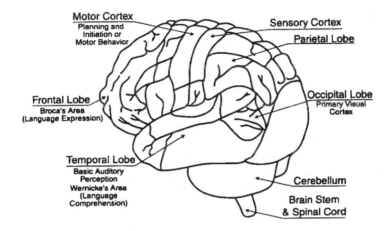

Motor Cortex
Planning and
Initiation or
Motor Behavior

Sensory Cortex
Parietal Lobe

Frontal Lobe
Broca's Area
(Language Expression)

Occipital Lobe
Primary Visual
Cortex

Temporal Lobe
Basic Auditory
Perception
Wernicke's Area
(Language
Comprehension)

Cerebellum

Brain Stem
& Spinal Cord

information and memory. It recognizes objects and their uses. Spatial functions such as geometry, map reading, and mathematical reasoning operate in this lobe.

A recent study of Einstein's brain by scientists at McMaster University in Ontario, Canada, has revealed that his interior parietal lobe was 15% wider than normal on both sides. An article published in the *San Bernardino Sun* newspaper on June 18, 1999, stated that the scientists also found the groove that normally runs from the front of the brain to the back did not extend all the way. This may have provided more neurons in this area of the brain to establish connections that allowed Einstein to have greater and different ways of thinking.

The occipital lobe provides visual information and shape and color recognition. This is the primary visual processing area. Depth and motion perception reside here.

The frontal lobe is responsible for about one-half the volume of the brain. It is located close to the forehead. Human frontal lobes are exceptionally well developed and are important to direct the brain as a whole. It sends messages to muscles and glands and is responsible for voluntary movement. It is the area of goal-directed behavior, long-term planning, problem solving, critical thinking, and decision making. The primary motor cortex and planning and initiation of motor behavior are located in the back part of the frontal lobe. The frontal lobe regulates emotional states and judgment.

Humans are the only known form of life that have prefrontal lobes. The prefrontal lobe is part of the frontal lobe and is located right behind the high forehead. This is where the highest level of processing occurs. Synthesis and evaluation can take place in this part of the brain. It is the area where the brain can operate at its higher levels. It is the final part of the cortex to mature (Sylwester, 1995).

Humans are the only known species that have prefrontal lobes.

I often have my students put their hands on their foreheads to better understand the location of the prefrontal lobe. They can also touch their own brain stem and become more aware of its location and function.

It is important for educators to become more cognizant of the connections between the brain and learning. When students are not challenged to use their brains in ways that are engaging, the dendrites are not stimulated.

Individuals can cause neural pruning or shut down their ability to perceive information. Boredom, repetition, anger, anxiety, and frustration can all click off learning and slow down the processing of information. This often happens to students in school when their dominant intelligences or ways of processing are not actively engaged. For example, if a student processes predominantly using movement, and he or she is not allowed to move, the brain processes may diminish, which causes neural pruning.

To extend our neural network by neural branching, we need to create more synapses between nerve cells. Listening to Baroque music or music by Mozart may stimulate neural pathways that are important to cognitive knowledge. To encourage neural branching, we can help students develop hypothetical thinking. An example of hypothetical thinking is asking students questions like, "What would have happened to slavery if Abraham Lincoln had not been elected president of the United States when he was?" or "What would our country be like now if slavery still existed?"

Reversal thinking strategies highlight situations that might go unnoticed. For example, the questions, "What would it be like if your day were completely reversed, if you had dinner in the morning and breakfast in the evening and went to bed in the morning rather than in the evening? What would be different for you during the day and the night? Would anything in your daily routine change? Why or why not?"

There is a significant correlation between drawing and electrical activity in specific regions of the brain. A study done by Crist (1990) in her doctoral dissertation on brain electrical activity as a predictor of drawing ability in 3-year-old children indicated all young children should be given the opportunity to develop their own natural ability. They should be allowed to experiment with media in line with their developmental maturity.

Crist contended that young children's drawing efforts are constrained by cortical maturity. Neurologically immature children are less attentive and need more teacher-directed approaches to be able to maximize their learning. Neurologically mature children are more focused and self-directed, thus needing less teacher direction.

The ability to draw the human form and to copy designs requires the integration of visual motor skills and the cortical maturity to plan and monitor the drawing process itself. This requires integration of two different parts of the brain.

Differences in information processing were observed between 3-year-old girls who were good drawers and 3-year-old boys who were less-developed drawers. Girls showed more activity in the central cortex and right parietal lobe than boys.

Correlations between drawing and brain electrical activity were found in the frontal cortex, right and left posterior temporal lobe, right and left occipital lobe, right, central, and left parietal lobe, and right and left central and central cortex.

Most preschoolers scribble in a rather primitive fashion, yet speak in complete sentences. Drawing ability generally emerges in developmental stages and improves with age and experience. Advanced drawing ability in gifted young artists is not usually identified until they are of school age. Some advanced young drawers are severely language disabled. Whereas these functions operate in two different locations of the brain, it would be interesting to study whether or not both parts can develop at the same rate and speed.

Time and Learning

Time is a powerful component of learning. The passage of time is essential for the brain to encode a new skill. After learning a new skill such as riding a bike or a cognitive skill such as reading or doing multiplication or division, it takes several hours to permanently store the information in the memory of the brain. Short-term memory allows individuals to hold information for a short period of time while they determine its importance. Long-term memory depends on the ability to string together and access long sequences of related motor actions, turn them into automatic skills, and translate related objects or events into stories (Treays, 1995).

It takes 5 to 6 hours for the memory to move to a permanent storage site in the brain. There is a neural window of vulnerability when a new skill can be eroded from memory. If teachers attempt to teach too many new skills that rely on the same part of the brain during that 5- to 6-hour period, the skills will not be retained in long-term memory. Teachers need to be aware of this, because too often they attempt to teach several skills at once and then wonder why the students do not retain the information. For example, when teaching reading, if a teacher goes beyond one or two short vowel sounds and continues to add additional skills during the same day, students may not encode the skills in their brains. It is more effective to demonstrate the skill through several different methods that actively engage the students in the learning process.

---

*It takes 5 to 6 hours to permanently
store a skill in the brain. Do not try to
teach too many skills at once that rely
on the same part of the brain because the
information is not retained in long-term memory.*

There is an important relationship between learning motor skills and neural activity. Some people say that humans think as much as 20% faster when they are standing up. Why? For some individuals, standing increases the heart rate by 10 beats per minute. The increased heart rate stimulates activity in the brain.

As an activity in the classroom, have students take their pulse while they are sitting down. Record the time. Then ask them to stand up and again take their pulse and record the time. Ask students to run in place for 30 seconds and take their pulse one more time. Record the time again. Have them compare the three different times. Ask if there are differences in the times, and if so, why they are different.

Emotional Part of the Brain

The brain has two memory systems: one for ordinary facts and one for emotionally charged ones. Because emotions can be acted on independently from the rational mind, we must understand the interplay between the emotional part of the brain responsible for working memory and the memory system for ordinary facts. Strong emotions from the limbic system can shut down neural pathways. When individuals are emotionally upset, they cannot think properly because the emotional part of their brain has over-powered the rational part. We all have said at some time, "I cannot think straight because I am so upset." When our emotions in-crease, our rational thinking can decrease.

> *The brain has two memory systems,*
> *one for ordinary facts and one for*
> *emotionally charged ones.*

Goleman's book *Emotional Intelligence* (1995) and LeDoux's *The Emotional Brain* (1996) emphasized the important role emotions play in learning. When an emotional response is positively con-nected to a learning experience, the brain sends a message that this information is important and that the memory should retain it. If the emotion becomes threatening or too strong, the brain decreases the efficiency of the rational thinking part of the cerebral cortex, and learning and retention decrease.

> ### *When our emotions increase, our rational thinking decreases.*

According to Goleman, emotional intelligence is how we handle our emotions and relationships with other people. The emotional and cognitive centers of the brain continuously interact. The emotional centers often interfere with the prefrontal part of the brain. When students are distressed, the emotional centers of the brain impede academic success.

Teachers with strong emotional intelligence are able to perceive whether they are engaging individual students. Affective and motivational factors are very important in the learning process. Information must be packaged in a way that enables students to decipher information for themselves because this allows them to place data into their long-term memory.

The research currently being conducted on the brain will help individuals to better understand the powerful connections between the mind and the body, and the intricate network of the different parts of the brain. This new information needs to be closely monitored and integrated into educational theories of how individuals learn and process information.

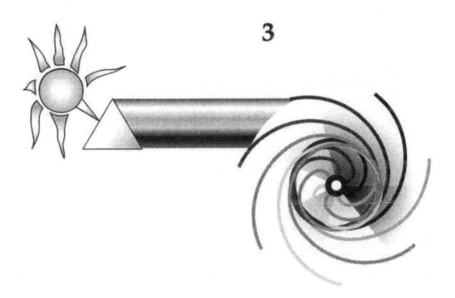

3

The Theory of Multiple Intelligences

Gardner argued that intelligence cannot be adequately assessed only by tests because paper-and-pencil measures are not always "intelligence fair." Gardner's theory contrasts markedly with the view that intelligence is based on a unitary or "general" ability for problem solving. Gardner introduced the theory of multiple intelligences in his book *Frames of Mind* (1983). This theory defines intelligence as an "ability to solve problems, or to create products that are valued within one or more cultures." According to Gardner, each individual possesses at least seven different intelligences, each with varied abilities. The seven intelligences are identified as linguistic, logical-mathematical, spatial, musical, bodily-kinesthetic, intrapersonal, and interpersonal. The following descriptions provide abbreviated examples of the characteristics of each.

Linguistic Intelligence

Linguistic students have highly developed auditory skills, enjoy reading and/or writing, like playing word games, have good memories for names, dates, and places, and prefer doing word processing on a computer. They may possess well-developed vocabularies and use language fluently, and are often able to spell words accurately and phonetically. They learn to read more effectively through a phonics approach.

LINGUISTIC INTELLIGENCE
- *Has highly developed auditory skills*
- *Enjoys reading and writing*
- *Has a good memory*
- *Spells words easily and accurately*
- *Uses language fluently*

Methods to which linguistically strong students can respond are lectures, word games, storytelling, advanced organizers, debate, speech, learning logs, reading aloud, and exercises that encourage reading, writing, spelling, and listening.

It is important to remember that not all students can perform at a high level with every one of the linguistic skills. Some students may be able to read and spell well, but not write well. Some students may not be able to process through listening only.

I am concerned with the strong emphasis on phonics only in our schools today. Students who do not process linguistically may have great difficulty learning to read if they are not taught in multidimensional ways with pictures, music, and movement.

TEACHING METHODS
- *Lectures*
- *Word games*
- *Storytelling*
- *Debates*
- *Speech*
- *Reading aloud*
- *Reading, writing, spelling, & listening exercises*

Teachers have a responsibility to identify the many different ways students learn so they can design a variety of teaching methods to reach all of them. We need to be careful to analyze each individual's abilities and not categorize them as strong in all linguistic areas when they may be strong only in certain ones.

Learning to read and express oneself is usually centered in the left hemisphere, but is triggered in two different areas of the brain. The structures in Wernicke's area in the temporal lobe, which links language and thought, and Broca's area in the frontal lobe, which processes grammatical structures and language expression, are connected through a bundle of nerve fibers called the arcuate fasciculus. These two structures develop at about age 2 and allow children to begin to speak in sentences (Sylwester, 1995).

Students who do not process linguistically should be taught in multidimensional ways with pictures, movement, and music.

Linguistic intelligence is probably the most universal of the seven intelligences because everyone learns to speak at an early age and most individuals learn to read and write. Linguistic intelligence includes several components: phonology (sounds of language), structure (syntax of language), semantics (appreciation of meaning), and the capacity to use language pragmatics (Armstrong, 1993).

The brain's ability to rapidly process linguistic information enhances the ability to think through and analyze complex problems. Sometimes linguistically strong individuals need to talk aloud and hear the sounds of their words to solve problems. Other individuals can formulate a story to recall related objects and events. This assists them in long-term memory (Sylwester, 1995).

Logical-Mathematical Intelligence

Logical-mathematical students like to explore patterns and relationships and are able to make connections. They enjoy doing activities in a sequential order, like mathematics problems; they enjoy conducting experiments to test things they do not understand; and they enjoy opportunities to problem solve and to reason logically, clearly, and scientifically. They learn best when information is presented in an orderly, logical, systematic way. They often process using deductive reasoning and prefer working with databases and spreadsheets on the computer.

LOGICAL-MATHEMATICAL INTELLIGENCE
- *Explores patterns and relationships*
- *Likes to problem solve and reason logically*
- *Follows sequential, logical directions*
- *Enjoys mathematics*
- *Uses experiments to test things out*

Methods that are appropriate for working with logical-mathematical learners are charting, graphing, listing, patterning, categorizing, sequencing, outlining, measuring, reasoning, solving problems, calculating, predicting, questioning, deciphering codes, and analyzing relationships.

TEACHING METHODS
- *Making charts, graphs, and lists*
- *Sequencing patterns and relationships*
- *Outlining*
- *Solving problems*
- *Calculating mathematically*
- *Predicting*
- *Questioning*
- *Categorizing*

I often like to discuss Fibonacci numbers when I explain logical-mathematical intelligence to students. Fibonacci numbers were discovered in the 12th century by Leonardo of Pisa, who was designing a formula to explain the breeding of rabbits. He wanted to discover how many pairs of rabbits would be in a pen after 12 months if one pair of rabbits produced a pair of babies at the beginning of each month.

The sequence can be explained by beginning with 1, the smallest Fibonacci number. The sequence is built by adding two numbers together to get the next number. If we add $1 + 0$, the sum equals 1. If we add $1 + 1$ together, we get 2. The next number in the sequence will be the sum of the previous two numbers. All positive integers can be represented either as a Fibonacci number or as the sum of nonadjacent (meaning not next to each other in the sequence) Fibonacci numbers. The Fibonacci sequence is 1, 1, 2, 3, 5, 8, 13, 21, 34, 55, 89, 144, and so on. Each of these numbers is the sum of the previous two numbers. The following table explains how the Fibonacci sequence works (Garland, 1987).

Fibonacci Sequence

1	
$1 + 0 = 1$	$13 + 8 = 21$
$1 + 1 = 2$	$21 + 13 = 34$
$2 + 1 = 3$	$34 + 21 = 55$
$3 + 2 = 5$	$55 + 34 = 89$
$5 + 3 = 8$	$89 + 55 = 144$
$8 + 5 = 13$	$144 + 89 = 233 \ldots$

This sequence is unusual because there are an infinite number of entries in the sequence and the numbers are reflected in many diverse places, such as in nature, art, architecture, music, poetry, science, mathematics, the stock market, and the human body. By presenting this information through practical applications of Fibonacci numbers, students become engaged in the learning process.

I often show my students pictures of the relationship of Fibonacci numbers to nature. For example, a sand dollar and a starfish are represented by the number 5. The inner core of an apple is divided into five segments, a lemon into eight, and a chile into three.

A giant sunflower spirals out from the center with 89 rows of seeds going one way and 55 rows of seeds going the other. Most pinecones have rows of bracts that spiral around 13 one way and 8 the other, although some pinecones spiral around 13 both ways. An artichoke spirals eight rows one way and five the other. A pineapple can spiral parallel rows of scales of either 8, 13, or 21. All of these represent Fibonacci numbers.

If you study an equiangular spiral, you will see that it uses Fibonacci proportions. There are all kinds of equiangular spirals in nature. The horn of a sheep, the sea horse, the nautilus shell, a dying poinsettia leaf, a growing fern, a pinecone, the ocean waves, and even the galaxy are created by an equiangular spiral.

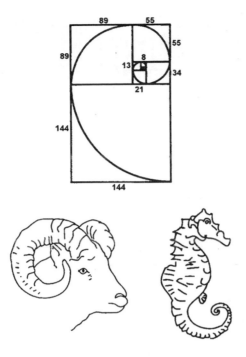

From a discussion of Fibonacci numbers and equiangular spirals in nature, students can be introduced to the golden ratio and how equiangular spirals appear in mathematics and architecture.

If you study the keys of the piano, you will note that an octave is 13 notes, 5 black keys and 8 white keys. The black keys are grouped in groups of 2s and 3s. It is interesting to note that 2, 3, 5, 8, and 13 are in the first group of Fibonacci numbers. There are three different types of scales: pentatonic, which is 5 notes; diatonic, which is eight notes; and chromatic, which is 13 notes. Songs like "Mary Had a Little Lamb" and "Go Tell It on the Mountain" are examples of pentatonic scales. "Row, Row, Row Your Boat" and "Are You Sleeping?" have eight notes and represent a diatonic scale. Modern symphonic music and jazz sometimes use a chromatic scale.

It is interesting that even in music we see the Fibonacci sequence at work. Fibonacci numbers are important to many aspects of the natural harmony that operates throughout the universe.

Spatial Intelligence

Spatial students enjoy art activities, read maps, charts, and diagrams, and think in images and pictures. They are able to visualize clear images about things and can complete jigsaw puzzles easily. They often need to see pictures before they can comprehend the meaning of words. Pictures can provide contextual clues to words and assist students to learn to read and spell. Spatial students can recognize relationships between objects.

SPATIAL INTELLIGENCE
- *Enjoys art activities*
- *Reads maps, charts, and diagrams*
- *Thinks with images and pictures*
- *Does jigsaw puzzles*

Methods for engaging spatial learners are to provide any type of visual clues such as pictures, computer graphics, slides, diagrams, posters, graphs, movies, mind maps, graphic organizers, and color markers or pens that allow the students to use different colors to denote different words or letters.

TEACHING METHODS

- *Pictures*
- *Slides*
- *Diagrams*
- *Posters*
- *Graphics*
- *Movies*
- *Mind maps*
- *Colors to represent words or letters*

Spatial learners may take notes in class by drawing pictures to retain the content. Students can learn to spell by seeing a picture of the word they are to learn and writing the correct spelling of the word several times within their own picture. This is very effective. Every time these students hear that word, they see the picture of the word and inside the picture is the correct spelling. This recall image enables them to translate that image of the word to the written page.

I actually taught an entire fourth grade class how to spell the word "geography" by using this method. To assist them in understanding what the word "geography" meant, I showed them locations on several maps. I then asked them to draw a picture they believed would depict the word "geography." Then I put the correct spelling on the board and asked them to copy the word correctly by placing it within their picture several times. Within 5 minutes, all but one student in the class had spelled it correctly. That student had made a mistake copying the correct spelling from the board. When I had him correct the spelling, I asked him to draw another picture and then place the correct spelling of the word several times within his new picture. This time he was able to spell the word correctly and the entire class applauded. The class was very excited they had accomplished this task so quickly.

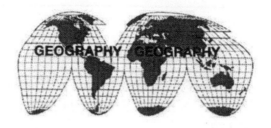

I knew to try this method because the entire class had taken the *Teele Inventory for Multiple Intelligences* (1992) and I had looked at their results and noted that almost all of the students were spatially strong. This approach to teaching spelling works with students who are strong spatially, but may not work as effectively with students who are not.

Musical Intelligence

Musical students are sensitive to the sounds in their environment, enjoy music, and may prefer listening to music when studying or reading. They appreciate pitch, rhythm, and timbre, and often sing songs to themselves or create their own melodies, rhythms, or rhymes. They understand the structure of music and can hear tonal sounds. When musical students clap their hands, snap their fingers, chant words, or move rhythmically, the rhythm can be used to engage them in the learning processes and to activate the musical part of the brain. Through this process, they are able to retain and apply information. They can learn phonics through rhythms and songs.

MUSICAL INTELLIGENCE
- *Sensitive to sounds in their environment*
- *Enjoys music*
- *Listens to music when studying and / or reading*
- *Sings songs*
- *Taps or hums rhythms*

The sounds of the letters can be taught by singing the letters of the alphabet to the tune of nursery rhymes. For example, "t is the sound of t, turtle, time, and tea" can be sung to the tune of "Old MacDonald's Farm."

Teaching techniques that are appropriate to musical learners are chants, clapping and snapping fingers to a beat, poetry such as haiku, limericks, couplets, and cinquains, rhyming words, and using music to demonstrate a concept or idea. I have used the music from *Chemistry Songbag* (Offutt, 1990) to teach chemistry concepts. I have also used the musical tape and book from *The Rainforest* (Nayer, 1993) to introduce information about the rainforest. One side of the tape reads a story linguistically and the other side sings a song about the rainforest musically. Songs about the alphabet can introduce students to each sound and letter. The book, *Chicka, Chicka, Boom, Boom* (Martin, 1989), comes with an audio cassette and provides a rhythmic way to teach the letters of the alphabet. Teachers and students can set up the sounds of the alphabet to simple melodies like "Row, Row, Row Your Boat," "Old MacDonald Had a Farm," and "Mary Had a Little Lamb." Students can create rhythms out of words or beat rhythms with instruments, hands, or a stick. They can write raps that describe what they are learning.

TEACHING METHODS

- *Chants*
- *Clapping and snapping fingers*
- *Poetry*
- *Music that matches the curriculum*
- *Moving rhythmically*

Background music can be used to relax or stimulate students. Baroque music is relaxing and is similar in beat to the heart. Music from the Olympics can provide inspiration and motivation to students. I have made a very powerful presentation by showing a picture of Van Gogh's painting *Starry, Starry Night* while playing Don MacLean's song "Vincent," which describes Van Gogh's life lyrically. This multimedia presentation provides an extremely moving experience because the words in the song depict aspects of the painting that can be seen spatially. The song "Hero" sung by Mariah Carey or Bette Midler can be used to introduce a writing or history lesson that describes heroes. *The Green Book* (Green, 1995) provides titles of music by category. I have recently discovered that music can engage students in the learning process by appealing to both the rational and the emotional parts of the brain simultaneously.

> *Music can engage students in the learning process by appealing simultaneously to both the rational and the emotional parts of the brain.*

I encourage teachers to show their students how to use coffee stirrers to beat out rhythms on their arms while they are studying. This technique has proven to be very successful with students because it makes no noise, but allows them to maintain a rhythm or beat while they work. This activity engages the musical area of the brain, which enables musically intelligent students to remain more focused, yet does not create a disturbance that tapping with a pencil or pen on their desks would.

Bodily-Kinesthetic Intelligence

Students who are bodily-kinesthetic, process knowledge through bodily sensations and use their bodies in unique and skilled ways. They need opportunities to move and act things out, and tend to respond best in classrooms that provide physical activities and hands-on learning experiences and that allow them to use manipulatives or to conduct experiments.

> *BODILY-KINESTHETIC INTELLIGENCE*
> - *Processes information through body sensations*
> - *Requires hands-on learning*
> - *Moves and acts things out*
> - *Uses body in unique and skilled ways and is often well coordinated*

Bodily-kinesthetic intelligence involves several parts of the brain; the ganglia at the base of each hemisphere, which coordinate the sensory and motor systems; the amygdala in the limbic system, which provides the emotional reaction for movements; the motor cortex, which codes movements and positions; and the cerebellum, which coordinates automatic movement (Sylwester, 1995).

TEACHING METHODS
- *Manipulatives*
- *Games*
- *Simulations*
- *Laboratory experiments*
- *Movement*
- *Hands-on activities*
- *Action-packed stories*

Methods for engaging bodily-kinesthetic intelligence in the classroom are to use manipulatives, hands-on activities, games, simulations, laboratory experiments, and action-packed stories; to act out information; and to move or to build background sets. If possible, a bodily-kinesthetic area should be created in every classroom regardless of grade level. This area is a place within the room where students can go when they cannot sit still. A rocking chair or bean bags could be located in this area.

Establish a bodily-kinesthetic area in the classroom.

I personally try to establish a bodily-kinesthetic area for every presentation I give because I have learned that adults, like students, do not prefer to sit all day. It is interesting to observe that some teachers in each group will simply stand in the bodily-kinesthetic area several times during the presentation.

There is no research that I can find that equates sitting to learning, so I do not believe it is necessary to remain seated the entire time an individual is engaged in the learning process. I personally am not able to sit for long periods of time and find that my brain will downshift if it is not constantly engaged in movement.

> *For long-term memory to occur with bodily-kinesthetic students, the brain has to be activated through movement.*

When I give presentations, I have participants demonstrate how to learn about circumference, diameter, and radius of a circle, and area and perimeter of a rectangle by using their bodies as a group. Bodily-kinesthetic intelligent students can comprehend what this means because of active participation. Students can spell out words and sentences, and can make the shape of a letter of the alphabet with their bodies. This seems to trigger several parts of their brain and they are better able to retain the information in long-term memory.

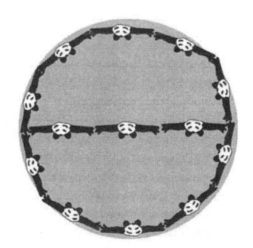

Chemistry symbols can be portrayed with the body and students can also act out historical, literary, artistic, musical, mathematical, or scientific figures with their bodies.

Because many students in both elementary and secondary classrooms are bodily-kinesthetic, educators need to allow students to move around more in the classroom.

Personally, I have noticed that I must have movement to focus or concentrate for long periods of time. I may twitch, tap, or shake some part of my body or move my fingers constantly or put things in my mouth. This is an effort to continually activate my brain and allow me to remain seated for long periods of time. I am also an individual who works on several projects at the same time, sometimes in different rooms of my home. I have found that by moving back and forth from room to room I am able to keep actively engaged and focused. I know that many students in our educational system are very much like me and also need to have some movement to keep them engaged in learning. When they are not allowed to move, they shut down and are unable to perform at their potential because of lack of activity.

Intrapersonal Intelligence

Intrapersonal students prefer their own inner world, like to be alone, are aware, and evaluate their own strengths, weaknesses, and inner feelings. They often have a deep sense of self-confidence, independence, and a strong will, and motivate themselves to do well on independent study projects. They may respond with strong opinions when controversial topics are being discussed. They like keeping a journal, prefer to work in quiet, independent settings, and are often self-reflective.

I have observed that some of the greatest power struggles teachers have are with students who are strong intrapersonally. These students often do not confide in individuals unless a feeling of trust has been established. If teachers or adults invade their private space too quickly, they may be met with great resistance. It is essential to create a nonthreatening, trusting environment in classrooms so that intrapersonal students feel comfortable. It is important to assist students to develop a more positive self-esteem or self-concept and to provide opportunities for them to focus more on their strengths and positive attributes.

Interpersonal Intelligence

Interpersonal students enjoy being around people, often have many friends, and participate in social activities. They create and maintain long-term relationships. They learn best by relating and participating in cooperative or collaborative group environments.

These students express empathy for the feelings of others, respond to their moods and temperaments, and can understand other perspectives. Interpersonal students prefer studying in groups and like to discuss information with others.

I believe it is essential to develop both of the personal intelligences within students because as adults they often will be placed in situations where they need to be able to switch from intrapersonal to interpersonal intelligence quickly. It is important for students to develop the ability to relate interpersonally and work collaboratively and cooperatively with others while also being able to reflect independently and to work alone.

Gardner (1983) stated that individuals are capable of processing information in at least seven different ways, but each individual varies in the degree of skill in each of the seven intelligences.

Individuals vary in the way they
process information.

Relationship between Personal Intelligences and Emotional Intelligence

If we examine the relationship between Goleman's (1995) emotional intelligence and Gardner's (1983) intrapersonal and interpersonal intelligences, we notice a close correlation between the two approaches. Emotional intelligence skills include self-awareness, empathy toward others, the ability to manage the emotions of both oneself and others, and an optimistic view of life. Goleman stated that emotional intelligence links the limbic and cognitive parts of the brain together to work in harmony. There is a strong relationship between thought and feeling. For individuals to optimize their intelligences, they must be placed in an environment that nurtures and encourages them to develop their potentials. The earlier that students gain insights into how they learn, the greater is the opportunity that they have to develop their cognitive and creative abilities.

Both Gardner and Goleman stated that it is not enough to focus only on literacy and numeracy in school because then educators lose sight of the complete intellectual and emotional capacity of students. Students must also be allowed to learn how to develop both their intrapersonal and their interpersonal abilities if they are to be adequately prepared with a basic emotional aptitude to manage their own lives and are to learn how to integrate both the emotional and cognitive centers of the brain.

Naturalist Intelligence

Gardner (1996) introduced an eighth intelligence, which he called the naturalist intelligence. He defines the naturalist as one who is able to recognize, categorize, and classify flora and fauna, who listens to and hears the sounds of the environment, who enjoys being outdoors, who notices relationships in nature, who sees connections and patterns with the plant and animal kingdom, and who is in tune with and explores nature. The naturalist enjoys interacting with a variety of living creatures and can discern differences among plant and animal species. The naturalist explores the relationship between nature and civilization. Gardner mentions that occupations such as hunter, fisher, farmer, gardener, and biologist are all related directly to the naturalist intelligence.

> # *NATURALIST INTELLIGENCE*
> - *Recognizes, categorizes, and classifies flora and fauna*
> - *Sensitive to sounds in their environment*
> - *Enjoys being outdoors*
> - *Interacts with plants and animals*

The notion of naturalist intelligence has prompted me to explore a new way to consider the concept of multiple intelligences because I feel that this intelligence overlaps several of the other seven, namely, logical-mathematical, spatial, musical, bodily-kinesthetic, and intrapersonal intelligences. I do believe that individuals such as James Audubon, John Muir, Luther Burbank, and Charles Darwin possessed attributes of the naturalist intelligence, but I view this intelligence as an intelligence that builds on some of the characteristics of the other seven. I will discuss this further in Chapter 5.

Basic Principles of Multiple Intelligences

The basic principle of multiple intelligences is that individuals have abilities in addition to the linguistic and logical-mathematical ones typically measured by intelligence tests. These abilities enable individuals to solve problems or to fashion products valued in the larger society (Gardner, 1983).

Gardner's theory states that individuals vary in their capabilities and ways of processing information. For example, individuals with musical intelligence excel more if they are provided with activities that utilize rhythms or some form of music. Those individuals who possess strong logical-mathematical skills become more engaged if information is presented in a logical, sequential, orderly manner.

> *Individuals utilize certain combinations of intelligences to perform different tasks.*

Gardner (1983) stated that individuals have a set of specific intelligences that are biopsychological potentials. These intelligences or abilities exist in the context of other abilities or knowledge. Individuals utilize certain combinations of intelligences to perform different tasks. For example, driving a car requires a combination of bodily-kinesthetic, spatial, intrapersonal, and often logical-mathematical and interpersonal intelligences. It is important to develop the dominant as well as less dominant intelligences because of the need to use them in different combinations daily to engage in a multitude of activities.

All of the intelligences can be developed more fully when positive educational and environmental circumstances exist. Biological potential or determination for learning and cognition remains only that until the environmental experiences permit that potential to function, develop, and flourish. For example, individuals who possess great ability in bodily-kinesthetic intelligence may not become great athletes unless they practice diligently and have supportive coaches who recognize their capabilities.

> *All of the intelligences can be developed more fully when positive educational and environmental circumstances exist.*

Philosophies consistent with multiple intelligences emphasize that people have diverse abilities or ways of learning, and different ways of demonstrating them (Gardner, 1991). The theory of multiple intelligences ascribes value to various abilities or intelligences that schools have often ignored, intelligences other than linguistic and logical-mathematical (Blythe and Gardner, 1990). For example, Pat Bolanos (1990), the principal of the Key School in Indianapolis, argues that all the intelligences are equally important in her school. Her school's philosophy is that all children can be provided with an equitable education. The school's purpose is to reach the entire spectrum of intelligences by offering instruction in music, dance, visual arts, computers, and foreign language in addition to the basic skills of reading, writing, spelling, listening, and mathematics.

Gardner (1983), in developing the theory of multiple intelligences, studied both experimental psychology and applied areas of intelligence. To formulate his theory, he drew on diverse sources of evidence instead of relying primarily on psychometric data. These sources included developmental psychology, neuropsychology, biology, and anthropology. He considered each candidate intelligence against eight criteria:

1. Its potential to be isolated in cases of brain damage
2. Its existence in special populations such as prodigies, idiot savants, and other exceptional individuals
3. The identification of core information processing mechanisms associated with the intelligence
4. The presence of a characteristic developmental pathway and a set of expert end states
5. An evolutionary history and evolutionary plausibility
6. Support from experimental psychology that reveals relative autonomy for the ability
7. Whether statistical analyses indicate a separate factor for the ability
8. Whether the ability has been encoded in a symbol system

According to Gardner not all of the intelligences meet every criterion, but all meet most of them (Gardner, 1983).

Multiple Intelligences Schools

Gardner's theory has received wide attention within educational circles where finding ways for all students to learn is a primary concern. The Key School, a public elementary magnet school in Indianapolis, was founded in 1987 based on multiple intelligences theory. Green Tree East Elementary School in Victorville became the first multiple intelligences school in California in 1991. Country Springs Elementary School, which is located in the Chino Unified School District in California, opened as a multiple intelligences school in 1993 and has experienced tremendous success both cognitively and affectively. Their academic achievement scores are very high and they have a 99.5% attendance rate because students want to attend school. Recently, on a statewide standardized test (the Stanford 9 test), Country Springs scored higher than all other elementary schools in their district and were at least 20% above the statewide average in all grade levels. They also have very few discipline problems because their students are actively engaged in learning methods that match how they learn.

> ## *When students are actually engaged in learning, they do not misbehave.*

Individual schools and districts all over the country and in many other countries as well have become interested in developing methods for integrating the theory of multiple intelligences into curriculum, instruction, and assessment measures.

Gardner (1997) has expressed concern that even the most outstanding students in the best schools in America just go through the motions of education. He believes an absence of understanding exists in schools. Many students are unable to take knowledge and skills and apply them successfully in new situations. Gardner suggested that the definition of excellence rests on high-level performance of understanding, which requires students to apply facts, skills, and knowledge successfully to complex problems in cognitive domains not previously experienced.

Not all students can learn in the same way and on the same day, and teachers should learn how to adapt their teaching methods to the way in which their students learn and process information. Teachers who acknowledge all of the intelligences as legitimate ways to learn can encourage students to engage and use their

> ## *Not all students can learn in the same way and on the same day.*

strengths as springboards for translating from one intelligence to another.

> *Teachers who acknowledge all of the intelligences as legitimate ways to learn can encourage students to engage and use their strengths as springboards for translating from one intelligence to another.*

In the past few years, several studies have shown how the theory has been used with certain populations, subject areas, or schools (Bouton, 1997; Gardner & Hatch, 1989; Hoerr, 1994; Kornhaber, 1997; Nefsky, 1997; Roesch, 1997; Smagorinsky, 1991). Implications for educational practices may also be drawn from multiple intelligences. The theory is consistent with curricula that encourage students to draw on and develop diverse intellectual abilities. For example, the Key School in Indianapolis has classes that focus on each intelligence. Country Springs Elementary School is committed to the philosophy that all children are gifted and is dedicated to implementing multiple intelligences as an integral part of all instruction.

Another possibility is a project-based curriculum. Gardner (1990) noted that well-designed projects draw on a variety of intellectual abilities. Interdisciplinary curricula similarly afford students opportunities to draw upon many intelligences.

There is no one pedagogy or curriculum method that will work effectively in all classrooms and with all students. In our educational system we should acknowledge the psychometric approach to intelligence, as well as incorporate the developmental progressions of individuals, the neurobiological information we are learning about the brain, and the concept of multiple measures of intelligence. When we do so, we will discover the untapped potential of all our students. We will increase student achievement and provide opportunities for our students to process information at much higher levels of thinking.

> *There is no one pedagogy or curriculum method that will work effectively in all classrooms and with all students.*

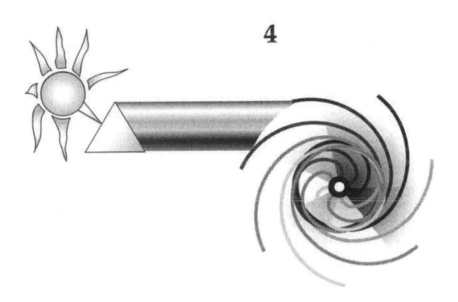

4

Changing Our Thinking About Education

The recent release of the *Third International Mathematics and Science Study* (TIMSS; U.S. Department of Education, 1996), which reported on cross-national comparisons of student achievement in mathematics and science, curricula, textbooks, and teacher practices for a range of 20 to 50 countries, depending on the particular comparison, supports the need to expand our educational paradigm and to analyze, evaluate, and more effectively understand beliefs and practices that have been the foundation of the American educational system for over 100 years.

Analysis of this study indicates a need to reflect on America's educational past and consider alternatives that will reshape the future. Albert Einstein is quoted as saying, "The world we have created is a product of our thinking. It cannot be changed without changing our thinking" (Calaprice, 1996). It is time for us to change the way we think about our educational system, to reflect more on how our students learn, and to reevaluate what and how much we should teach. As our nation moves toward a more standard-based system, current information on the neurobiology of the brain and the ways individuals process information must be integrated into this new system if we are to ultimately improve student achievement.

We must provide the best education possible to prepare our students for the 21st century. To be ready for an increasingly complex, everchanging, technological society, our students must possess a higher skill base that allows them to think, analyze, apply, evaluate, and synthesize information. Bloom (1956) provided a taxonomy of educational objectives for educators. This taxonomy progresses from knowledge, to comprehension, to application, to analysis, to synthesis, to evaluation. During this process, learners produce something unique or derive a set of abstract relations that builds to the highest level. Evaluation requires judgments of both internal evidence and external criteria. Our students must be able to process at the higher levels of Bloom's taxonomy, not remain only at the knowledge or comprehension level.

> *We must provide the best education possible to prepare our students to be successful in the 21st century.*

Future Workforce

The future workforce will require the students of tomorrow to do more than read, write, speak, listen, and perform mathematical computation. Students will need to develop skills that provide opportunities to think creatively, make decisions and judgments, solve problems independently, reason, envision new ideas and products, and know how they learn and how others who could assist them learn.

> *The future workforce will require students to think at higher levels and to envision new ideas and products that have not previously been designed.*

Because many of our students will be working in their homes on their computers, they will need to possess additional personal qualities that require them to manage their time independently, have integrity, and be able to take individual responsibility for their work. They will be required to utilize both intra- and interpersonal intelligences at the same time, by developing the ability to work independently some of the time and to relate interpersonally at other times. They will need to switch back and forth between the two personal intelligences all the time.

Technological competence has become an additional basic skill that will be required of all individuals entering the workforce. It is absolutely essential that all of our students become technologically literate by the time they leave our schools; they will be required to know word processing skills, database and spreadsheet skills, and the ability to research information on the Internet.

"Education should not be looked upon as the mere acquisition of academic subject matter, but as a part of life itself." —John Dewey

Dewey (1902) said, "Education should not be looked upon as the mere acquisition of academic subject matter, but as a part of life itself." The TIMSS report supports this statement: it found that those countries that scored the highest were the ones that presented academic content matter in realistic and practical ways. The study indicated that many of our students are not receiving the science and mathematics education that will allow them to achieve at their optimal levels. The study also reflected the time devoted to mathematics and science instruction, the content covered, student access to that content, and instructional practices in science and mathematics.

The National Commission on Teaching and America's Future (1996) report "What Matters Most: Teaching for America's Future" indicates that fewer than 10% of high school students can read, write, compute, and manage scientific material at the high levels required in today's and tomorrow's workforce. Most schools are unable to produce students who are prepared for the 21st century because they have not been taught to process information at the higher levels of Bloom's taxonomy.

> *Our educational system should be incorporating current knowledge of how students learn, recent research on the brain, and ways to effectively teach all students.*

Methods for teaching students in a variety of ways and having them demonstrate what they know through multiple measures of assessment must be emphasized at every grade level if we are to have all our students experience higher academic achievement.

Focusing primarily on the psychometric approach could be a big mistake if our nation wants to create experiences that produce effective success in learning. Students of today have a wider range of learning needs—some have language needs, some learn in different ways than currently taught, and others have learning disabilities. To accommodate these diverse students, our educational system should be incorporating the current knowledge of how students learn, recent research on the brain, and ways to effectively teach all students. We all, as parents, teachers, administrators, school board members, community members, business people, and elected officials, need to become more aware of the many different ways our students are able to understand information, and then collaborate with and assist each other to make the changes that will improve our educational system for all students.

The TIMSS report revealed that the more years U.S. students are in school, the more their achievements experience a downward trend in comparative mathematics and science achievement. Students in 4th grade were in the middle range, ranked 29 out of 41 countries in mathematics and in the top 4 countries in science. Between 4th and 8th grade, the United States was the only country that had a drop in scores. That drop continued through 12th grade.

Teele Inventory for Multiple Intelligences

The *Teele Inventory for Multiple Intelligences* (TIMI), an instrument I created in 1992, is a forced-choice pictorial inventory that contains 56 numbered pictures of panda bears that represent characteristics of each of the seven intelligences and that provides individuals with 28 opportunities to select between two choices. The different intelligences are matched with one another and students have eight different opportunities to select each of the seven intelligences. The maximum possible points for each intelligence is 8. Individuals are asked to select one of the two choices

1A   1B

that they feel is the most like them. There are no right or wrong answers. The inventory is one of the ways to identify the dominant intelligences each individual possesses. The TIMI has been utilized in a broad spectrum of applications from preschool to universities. The results of the inventory indicate that students process information in many different and diverse ways using different combinations of the intelligences.

My work with the *Teele Inventory for Multiple Intelligences* has indicated that students' selections of pictures that reflect linguistic and logical-mathematical intelligences declines the longer they are in school.

After analyzing the TIMSS data and conclusions, and reflecting on my own research, I offer a suggestion as to a possible piece in the puzzle of why our students decline in achievement after fourth grade.

An analysis of over 6,000 answer sheets has revealed some data that indicate we may want to examine the manner in which we present instruction at different grade levels. The mean scores demonstrate that at the primary level both male and female students are interested in linguistic and logical-mathematical intelligences, but as they advance to the upper grades that interest declines. Based on results of this inventory, the older the students become, the less they prefer to learn in those two ways and the more they desire active, interpersonal and visual ways of learning.

A Student Profile of Multiple Intelligences Based on the
Teele Inventory of Multiple Intelligences

	Primary	Upper	Middle School	High School
Linguistic	4.09	3.48	2.73	2.74
Logical-mathematical	4.05	3.66	3.04	2.86
Spatial	4.76	4.89	4.83	4.52
Musical	3.32	3.84	3.82	3.66
Bodily-kinesthetic	4.39	4.75	4.76	4.98
Intrapersonal	3.39	2.95	3.26	3.54
Interpersonal	3.93	4.39	5.48	5.58

SOURCE: Teele, S. (1992). *Teele Inventory for Multiple Intelligences*. Used with permission.

The scores in the table on this page indicate that students at all grade levels respond to spatial and bodily-kinesthetic intelligences in their selections on the inventory.

As we reevaluate our educational system, the developmental progression of students and the different ways they process information should become strongly embedded in both curriculum and assessment measures.

Gender Comparison of Student Responses to the *Teele Inventory for Multiple Intelligences*

When I was conducting my research, I also did a gender comparison. The gender study demonstrated differences in the ways males and females process information beginning in fourth grade. The mean scores indicate that males tend to process stronger in logical-mathematical and spatial intelligences, whereas females process stronger with linguistic intelligence. At each grade level, the mean scores varied.

It is important that educators better understand the unique developmental progressions of students by age and grade level as different ways to improve our educational system are considered.

The gender data are supported by Halpern and Crothers (1997), who state that numerous studies in the last 10 years have indicated that females, on average, score higher on tasks that require access to and use of phonological and semantic information in the long-term memory, verbal fluency and writing ability, production and comprehension of complex prose, perceptual speed, fine motor tasks, and decoding nonverbal communication. Females often have more developed fine motor skills. They tend to process interpersonally and by verbalizing aloud to others or to themselves to solve problems. Females have demonstrated greater ability in the somatosensory areas of touch, taste, hearing, and odor, as well as speech articulation. They are able to better interpret emotions and tend to be more nurturing and effective at arbitrating differences between individuals. They also receive higher grades in school. Jensen (1995) found that females hear better, which enables them to speak earlier and learn languages more quickly.

The Seven Intelligences by Gender and Grade Level

	Grade 1		Grade 4		Grade 7		Grade 9		Grade 12	
	Male	Female	Male	Female	Male	Female	Male	Female	Male	Female
Linguistic	3.90	4.06	3.64	4.09	2.52	2.92	2.78	3.21	2.40	3.28
Logical-mathematical	4.25	4.33	4.28	3.47	3.37	2.54	3.78	3.09	3.16	2.26
Spatial	4.81	4.62	5.21	4.46	5.27	4.51	4.72	4.10	4.95	4.22
Musical	3.22	3.50	3.55	4.37	3.76	3.91	3.33	3.36	3.73	3.95
Bodily-kinesthetic	4.36	3.88	4.46	4.66	4.56	4.89	4.65	5.06	4.64	4.95
Intrapersonal	3.53	3.70	2.81	3.11	3.08	3.48	3.40	3.50	3.55	3.79
Interpersonal	3.80	3.90	4.05	3.83	5.32	5.63	5.18	5.57	5.48	5.48

SOURCE: Teele, S. (1992). *Teele Inventory for Multiple Intelligences*. Used with permission.

Males, on average, score higher on tasks that require transformations in visual-spatial working memory, tasks that involve moving objects, motor skills involved in spatio-temporal responding, and fluid reasoning, especially in abstract mathematical and science domains. Males can see things mentally in three-dimensional formats and have better distance vision and depth perception than females. Males obtain higher scores on standardized tests that are designed to predict grades in college and graduate school, yet females receive higher grades than males.

These studies support the findings that females, on average, are more linguistic and interpersonal, and males, on average, are more logical-mathematical and spatial. Each gender exhibits different strengths in the bodily-kinesthetic area, which supports the close mean scores I found on the TIMI inventory. Both genders were strong in that area.

Halpern (1992) and Halpern and Crothers (1997) indicated that some studies also revealed that males were overrepresented in the areas of mental retardation, attention disorders, dyslexia, stuttering, and delayed speech. Perhaps this is because they develop linguistically later than females and our educational system does not account for that fact. I believe that sometimes males are classified as attention deficit when they really are only processing bodily-kinesthetically and must have some form of movement to keep them engaged in the learning process. They are placed into rigid classroom routines before they are ready and are not allowed to move around when they become restless. Because they find it difficult to sit still, their behavior is often labeled as hyperactive when all they really need is to be in classrooms that provide opportunities for them to move around.

Research such as the TIMSS report indicates there are many cognitive areas in which the genders differ and many areas in which there were no significant differences. TIMSS revealed that boys in about 75% of the 41 countries with data from eighth grade did significantly better than girls in science. In mathematics, they led in about 15% of the nations tested (U.S. Department of Education, 1996). In no country did girls significantly outperform boys in mathematics and science (Vogel, 1996).

Perhaps a model should be considered that is based on variables that are both biological and social and, therefore, cannot be

> ## *Learning is both a socially mediated event and a biological one.*

classified into one of these two categories. Learning is both a socially mediated event and a biological one. Individuals are unique in the ways they learn. Some are able to learn certain subject areas quicker than others. Learning depends on what is already known and on the neural structures that affect learning. Psychological, biological, social, and environmental factors may all contribute to guiding the learning process. Do we in education consciously consider all these factors when we design individualized educational plans for each student? I do not believe we do, and this is an area that needs to be addressed in every educational setting.

> ## *Psychological, biological, social, and environmental factors may all contribute to guiding the learning process.*

Many differences appear early in life. The visual-spatial short-term memory and mathematical ability appear as early as in preschool with males. Perceptual advantages in females appear early in infancy, and fluency differences are evident in the toddler years. The developmental progressions are different in males and females. Girls tend to mature earlier than boys, and this leads to males being miscategorized and placed in programs for the learning disabled in early years. Boys mature at a much slower rate throughout childhood (Shaywitz et al., 1995).

Whereas educators have become aware of the many different ways students learn, a question to be asked is why the focus is not initially on developing the areas in which students are strong, and then, secondarily, concentrating on the areas that are not as strong. This approach would enhance students' self-esteem and acknowledge their unique gifts and talents. Students could then be taught how to translate from their dominant intelligences to their less dominant intelligences. I have found that once students discover they can succeed in learning, they are much more willing to try harder.

Students can be taught how to translate from their dominant intelligences to their less dominant intelligences.

Classrooms that support all of the intelligences can assist students in developing both their stronger and weaker areas. Teachers should try to provide more flexibility and time to allow students to translate from their dominant ways of processing information to the areas they are struggling with, particularly in reading, writing, spelling, and mathematics. Multiple ways to measure ability and achievement must be used to counter the fact that males score higher on standardized tests than females.

Once students discover they can succeed in learning, they are more willing to try harder.

Study of the brain has revealed that there are differences in the shape of the corpus callosum between females and males. Females have a larger and more bulbous structure (Allen, Richey, Chai, and Gorski, 1991; Steinmetz, Stanger, Schluag, Huang, and Jancke, 1995). This research supports the theory that female brains are more bilaterally organized in their representation of cognitive functions (Jancke and Steinmetz, 1994). The difference in the shape of the corpus callosum implies better connectivity between the two cerebral hemispheres, on average, for females (Innocenti, 1994). Further studies may reveal that there are different patterns of activities in male and female brains when they engage in certain cognitive activities. Brain structures change due to age in response to both hormonal and environmental events. Neurons are modified through experience even in adulthood.

The question arises as to how much are the gender differences determined by socially mediated learning theories and how much by genetics. Baenninger and Newcombe (1989) discovered that participation in spatial activities is important in the development of spatial intelligence and that females engage in fewer spatial activities than males. Why is this? Is it because females have been socialized to participate in other activities and have not had the opportunity to develop spatial abilities, or are there really genetically established gender differences that are further magnified by different experiences provided to each sex?

> *We need to personalize instruction to accommodate the different ways students learn.*

Educators can provide opportunities for all students to improve on cognitive tests by seeing that they receive appropriate instruction. We do know that there are intellectual skills in which females excel and others in which males excel. Why is it that we do not personalize our instruction to accommodate these differences? The educational experience is very powerful in predicting the level of achievement in a cognitive domain.

At the adolescent level, peer group socialization has become a strong factor in social learning theory. The need for acceptance, that is, development of self-esteem during adolescence, is heavily influenced by peer groups, particularly same sex groups (Harris, 1995). This is why interpersonal intelligence is so dominant in both males and females at the secondary level. In my studies, it is one of the top two intelligences in both males and females in grades 7 to 12 (Teele, 1994).

In the psychobiological model, cause and effect can become circular. Structural and functional differences in the anatomy of the brain could both result from different environmental experiences and cause individuals to select different experiences from their environment. Ungerleider (1995) showed that changes in cortical representations occur after specific experiences, as demonstrated by brain imaging techniques. Perhaps it is possible to determine what experiences influence the branching of dendrites. Biological and environmental factors appear to be intertwined in ways that affect intelligence and learning. Individuals may unknowingly select experiences based on the motivational and expectancy factors of others.

> ***Biological and environmental factors are intertwined in ways that affect intelligence and learning.***

A multiple intelligences approach may assist us in defining the wiring or internal language of the way individuals process information. Everyone learns information individually in different, multipath sequences, using previous experience as the foundation to which more learning is added. We need to think of each individual's brain as unique, operating as its own individual computer.

There continue to be remarkable discoveries in research on the brain and how individuals learn. The changes engendered by these discoveries will greatly influence both our educational system and our future workforce. We must redesign our educational system to allow all students to develop their intellectual abilities to their full potential.

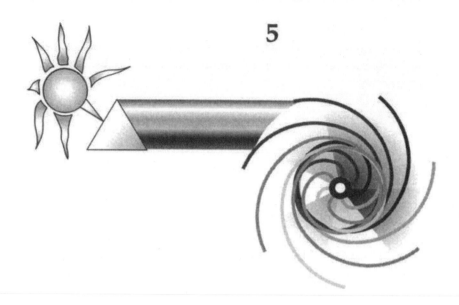

5

Rainbows of Intelligence Model

The rainbows of intelligence model has been created to build upon multiple intelligences and to address the complex pathways that enable individuals to process information. Educators need to understand the interrelationships among the intelligences and how they affect the unique ways in which all students learn.

The model compares the colors of the rainbow and primary, secondary, and complementary colors to the intelligences. There is an interesting analogy between colors, the rainbow, and how individuals learn. This will be explained by presenting a different way to conceptualize the theory of multiple intelligences.

What Is a Rainbow?

I believe we are all rainbows or spectrums of intelligences. A spectrum contains the seven distinct colors we can see, red, orange, yellow, green, blue, indigo, and violet, as well as other kinds of light, including ultraviolet and infrared, which we cannot see.

Ultraviolet light is adjacent to the violet end of the spectrum and has a shorter wavelength and higher energy. Infrared is adjacent to red and has a longer wavelength and less energy (Lawrence Hall of Science, 1989). Just like the color spectrum, there are seven distinct colors in the rainbow we can see, many other wavelengths we cannot see, and often secondary rainbows that are different combinations of the colors. They appear at different times and in different locations.

A rainbow is produced by sunlight passing through a collection of raindrops that spread that sunlight out into a spectrum of colors. Sunlight is made up of the whole range of colors that the eye can detect as well as light that the eye cannot detect. Ahrens (1994) defined a rainbow as a group of nearly circular arcs of color in the sky that occur when the sun's rays shine upon falling rain. These arcs have a common center, which is the "bow" part of the rainbow.

> *A rainbow is produced by sunlight passing through a collection of raindrops that spread the sunlight out into a spectrum of colors.*

Every rainbow is a full circle. However, the rainbow is seen as a bow or arc of different sizes at different times. The full circle of the arc cannot be seen from the ground because the earth gets in the way, but can be observed from an airplane. For a rainbow to become visible to the human eye, the sun must be behind the observer who is facing the falling rain. The rain is falling in one part of the sky, in the direction of the rainbow, and the sun is shining in another area. The center of the circular arc of the rainbow is in the direction opposite that of the sun.

> *Every rainbow is a full circle, but is seen as a bow or arc.*

A rainbow is created when rays of sunlight refract in and reflect off atmospheric water particles, which act as prisms. Sunlight appears colorless and is commonly called white light. However, it really comprises a mixture of different colors. We can only see these colors when light passes through a transparent substance, such as water or glass, which separates the colors into a rainbow pattern called the spectrum. The spectrum consists of visible light or colors that can be seen and radio waves, microwaves, gamma rays, infrared, ultraviolet, and X-rays that cannot be seen (MacMillan/McGraw, 1993).

Each color within the ray of white light is refracted at a different angle, forming successively wider bands of color. Together these bands produce a full spectrum. Spectra from many raindrops combine to form a circular pattern that results in a rainbow.

> *When a light ray enters or leaves a raindrop,*
> *it changes direction and the change is*
> *different for each color.*

According to physicists from the University of Illinois (1997), a rainbow is curved because of refraction in the drops of water. When a light ray enters or leaves a raindrop, it changes direction and the change is different for each color that makes up the sunlight. The size of the circle is different for each color and the light is separated into the colors of the rainbow.

The center of the circle is always at a point in the sky opposite the sun. The size of the visible portion of the rainbow depends on the altitude of the sun; it is largest when the sun is at the horizon. A rainbow cannot be seen when the altitude of the sun is greater than 42° because no part of it is above the horizon.

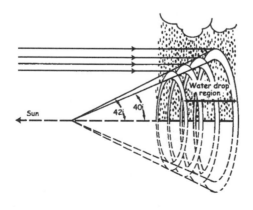

A typical raindrop is spherical. When a light ray strikes the surface of the raindrop, some light is refracted and some passes through the surface into the drop. The light beam reflects twice within the drop and this is the light the observer sees.

A rainbow is a whole continuum of colors from red to violet and even beyond the colors that the eye can see. It exhibits all the colors of the spectrum; the inner part is always violet and the outer part is red. The colors of the rainbow emerge because sunlight is made up of the entire range of colors the human eye can detect. The combined range of colors appears white to the eye. In 1666, Sir Isaac Newton determined that white sunlight contains all the visible colors of the spectrum (Lynds, 1997). He allowed a beam of sunlight to enter through a hole in his window blind and pass through a glass prism. The prism split the light into a band of colors on the wall. He called the band of colors a solar spectrum. He said that rays of light are bodies of different sizes.

> *Only one color of light can be seen from each raindrop. It requires many raindrops to see the colors in the rainbow.*

The colors on the inside of a rainbow appear brighter than those on the outside because raindrops refract light. The human eye can see only one color of light that is reflected from each raindrop; thus numerous raindrops are required to be able to see the spectrum of colors of a rainbow. The larger the raindrops, the brighter the rainbow's colors. Smaller raindrops produce rainbows of colors that overlap and appear almost white (Arizona State University, 1997).

Light shines on the half of each raindrop facing the sun. White light shining on the left side exits as a colored light on the right side, whereas white light shining on the right side exits on the left side of the raindrop as a colored light. This happens at every point on the sunward side of the raindrop and a circle of light is created from the incoming parallel light beams reflecting and refracting through the spherical surface. The refracted light from many raindrops contributes to form the rainbow. Raindrops lower in the sky contribute blue and green light; drops higher in the sky contribute red and yellow light (University of Illinois, 1997).

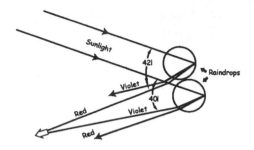

The different wavelengths or colors of the light in a rainbow spread out because of refraction. The reflected light is refracted as it exits the drop. Boyer (1959) stated that Descartes called this three-stage process the refraction–reflection–refraction pattern. The angle at which each color emerges from the raindrops in a rainbow is different, which enables the different colors to be seen. Red light is bent the least and exits the drop within an angle of 42° relative to incoming sunlight. Blue light emerges at 40.6°. Violet light is bent the most and emerges at an angle of 40°. Other colors leave the raindrops at angles somewhere between 40 and 42°. Much of the refracted light passes right through the drop and is not visible to the observer's eye at all (University of Illinois, 1997).

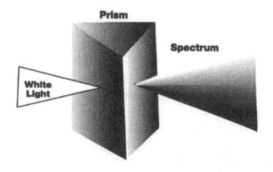

White light is composed of all the wavelengths of visible light. The waves that make up sunlight and incandescent light are a mixture of all the colors of the spectrum. If you break up the white light, you can see the various components of that light revealed as the spectrum of colors.

Special optical devices called prisms can split white light into its various wavelengths. This happens because the different colors in the white light respond to the glass in different ways. Blue light bends or refracts more than green light. Green light refracts more than the wavelengths that correspond to red light. This phenomenon is called dispersion and it occurs in all substances that refract light. As the sunlight shines into the water, the light is bent or refracted and broken up or dispersed. When the light reemerges from the other side, it travels in a different direction from its original path and is no longer just white light, but rather a spectrum of colors (University of Illinois, 1997).

When you see a rainbow, the sun is usually behind and above you, and the rain is in front of you or landing right on you. The sunlight bounces off the raindrops and reflects into your eyes. Even though the sunlight is primarily white light and is reflecting off the raindrops, the colors are present because the sunlight is reflecting off the raindrops as well as also refracting and dispersing in the raindrops. The raindrops act like a prism to split the white light from the sun into its component colors.

The raindrop is like a mirror that reflects some of the refracted light back toward the sun. These refracted rays are seen as a rainbow. No two raindrops are the same size, but rather a mixture of many sizes and shapes.

Our intelligences are like the spectrum of colors. Sometimes our intelligences are very obvious and sometimes they are not visible and are waiting to be discovered or activated.

Our students represent many different sizes, shapes, and ways of learning. Too often education does not reflect these differences. Sometimes in school we cannot see the refracted rays of our students and do not let their full colors shine. Because our educational system has for so many years been a system that recognizes only the linguistic and logical-mathematical learners, the mirrors in our school have not reflected many of the colorful and creative ways our students can learn.

> *When our students are given the opportunity*
> *to let their "lights shine," they reveal a full prism of*
> *colors or abilities that may never be discovered if*
> *they are not allowed to use their full spectrum*
> *of intelligences.*

Our ability to learn and process information involves both dominant and less dominant intelligences that work together. We use different combinations of intelligences to perform certain tasks. When our students are given the opportunity to let their "lights shine," they reveal a full prism of colors or abilities that may never be discovered if they are not allowed to use their full spectrum of intelligences.

The analogy of the rainbow and the individual raindrops applies to the learning process. Like each raindrop that falls, individuals processing information are unique. The brain sends signals to different parts of the hemispheres so that it can perform tasks. Some students process predominantly in the left hemisphere; others in the right. Neurons transmit across the hemispheres through the corpus callosum. If our brains process like the raindrops and each area of the brain represents a different raindrop, then it is necessary to combine and engage different parts of the brain to reach the full spectrum of human processing.

Each rainbow is your own. Because a rainbow is a special distribution of colors and is referenced to a definite point, no two observers see the same rainbow. Each eye sees a unique, individualized rainbow. A rainstorm is a three-dimensional object. Rain falls from one or more clouds onto an area on the ground. Only those raindrops within 42° of the line of sight reflect light back to the eye. Some raindrops reflect color, while most reflect white light straight back.

> *If each area of the brain represents a different*
> *raindrop, then it is necessary to combine different*
> *parts of the brain to reach the full spectrum of*
> *human processing.*

Sometimes we see a second rainbow on the outside of the first one, which is a brighter rainbow. This is called a secondary rainbow. A secondary rainbow occurs when raindrops high in the atmosphere refract and reflect light back to the viewer. These raindrops are higher than those that cause the primary rainbow and are different because they internally reflect the incoming sunlight twice rather than just once. The secondary rainbow's rays exit the raindrop at an angle of 50° rather than the 42° for the red primary bow. Blue light emerges at an even larger angle of 53°. The sunlight hits the bottom of the raindrop to make the secondary rainbow. There is still sunlight hitting the other parts of the raindrops. However, some of the light is transmitted through the raindrops without reflecting and some light is reflected and re-fracted but does not go directly into our eyes (Arizona State University, 1997). That light may be seen by others, depending on where they are standing.

> *Each rainbow is your own. Each eye sees a unique, individualized rainbow.*

The sequence of colors in the secondary rainbow is reversed compared to the primary rainbow. The primary rainbow's drops that are higher up contribute red light and the drops lower down contribute blue light. The secondary rainbow's drops that are higher up contribute blue light, while the lower drops contribute red light.

Two other types of rainbows not commonly known are reflection rainbows and lunar rainbows. A reflection rainbow is a combination of two rainbows that is produced by sunlight coming from two different directions: one directly from the sun; the other from the reflected image of the sun. The angles are different and the elevations of the arcs are also different. Sometimes a full moon is bright enough to allow light to be refracted by raindrops to form a lunar rainbow. Lunar rainbows are not as bright as those produced by sunlight and are not easy to observe.

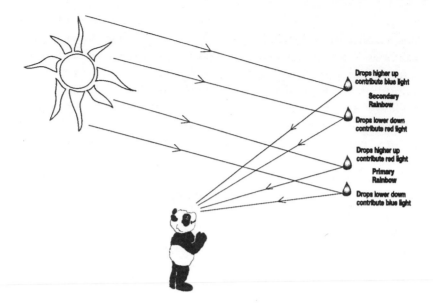

The beauty of the rainbow lies in the eyes of the beholder and the angle from which it is viewed. Could this physical phenomenon also have applications to the educational process?

The answer is "Yes, it could," as we observe how students learn. Sometimes intelligences like the colors are not easy to discover. We have to look with a more educated eye to see individuals' unique abilities for learning.

Gardner's seven intelligences may be compared to the seven colors of the rainbow. Many raindrops combine to form the rainbow and exhibit the colors of the spectrum. If we consider the human potential as the entire spectrum of the rainbow with seven different colors or seven different intelligences that can be seen

Each individual is unique and has the potential to develop each color of the rainbow or all of the intelligences by reflecting off several different raindrops or ways of learning.

and infinite combinations of colors that cannot always be seen by the human eye, then we realize that each individual is unique and has the potential to develop all of the intelligences by reflecting off several different raindrops or ways of learning.

Each raindrop represents one color, but together they act like a prism that allows each color to emerge at a different angle and enables us to see the different colors. Only when the sunlight reflects and refracts off the raindrops can you witness the colors. This applies to every individual. If we do not tap into the correct angle or manner of processing information, we often miss the opportunity to see the total rainbow of colors or the potential of each individual. Because we can only see one color from each raindrop, we need to have many raindrops to form the rainbow. If we address students using only one method of instruction or assessment, we may or may not tap into the dominant way or ways they process information. Too often our teaching methods create only white light in our students brains and do not trigger the rainbows of potential that tap into both sides of the brain.

> *If we do not tap into the correct angle or manner or processing for each individual, we cannot see the total rainbow of colors or the potential for each individual.*

Teachers can break up the perceived white light to reveal intelligences or colors not ordinarily discovered by providing opportunities for students to process using all of the intelligences. Because some intelligences are not as readily observed as others and may be hidden "higher in the sky," many different methods must be integrated into the curriculum to enable all of the intelligences to shine.

Primary, Secondary, and Complementary Colors

To completely understand this model for multiple intelligences, we need to examine the relationship of primary, secondary, and complementary colors to learning. There are two different ways to analyze primary colors: primary colors of light, which are additive colors, and primary colors of printing and paint, which are subtractive colors (Woolf, 1999).

Color reproduction is based on the theory of three-color vision. White light is composed of electromagnetic vibrations. The wavelengths of all light have three primary colors, red, green, and blue, and are called the primary colors of light. They are called additive primaries because when the lights of these colors are added together white light is produced. White light consists of varying wavelengths and contains all the visible colors in the spectrum. Each individual color is associated with a different wavelength.

The primary colors of light are the only colors that cannot be made from any other colors, but all other colors can be made from them. The three primary colors can produce a wider range of

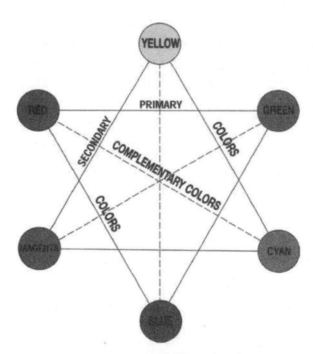

PRIMARY COLORS OF LIGHT

colors than any three other colors. No two primary colors can produce a third primary color.

If we blend two primary colors of light together, we create a secondary color. For example,

$$green + blue = cyan,$$

$$red + blue = magenta,$$

$$red + green = yellow.$$

The primary colors of printing and paint are cyan, magenta, and yellow (Woolf, 1999). These colors are called subtractive primary colors because each represents the two additive colors left after one primary color has been absorbed or subtracted from white light (Bruno, 1989). The subtractive colors of printing and paint can be mixed together in varying amounts to match almost any hue. If all three are mixed in equal amounts, they produce black (Woolf, 1997).

Cyan, magenta, and yellow are the ink colors used in the reproduction of color artwork, process printing, and photography. A fourth color, black, is generally added to reinforce the detail of the picture, enhance the modeling, and improve the reproduction of gray or neutral colors. This technique is called four-color process printing. The dots in process printing are placed next to each other to create the values between the four colors (Stone and Eckstein, 1983). A halftone negative is made for each color. When the negatives are made, the halftone screen is rotated to a different angle for each color. This change prevents the printed dots from interfering with each other.

Subtractive color mixing occurs when two primary colors overlap so that both objects subtract colors from white light. When two of the primary colors of light overlap, secondary colors, magenta, cyan, and yellow, appear and become the subtractive primary colors.

If we blend two primary colors of printing and paint, we create the following secondary colors:

$$yellow + magenta = red,$$

$$cyan + yellow = green,$$

$$cyan + magenta = blue.$$

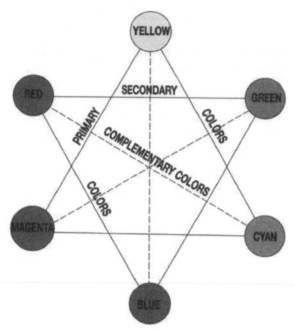

PRIMARY COLORS OF PRINTING AND PAINT

Complementary colors are any two colors that are opposite each other on the color wheel. The term "complementary" indicates a relationship between the two colors. When complementary colors of light are added together they produce white. Complementary colors of printing and paint are those two colors that produce black when overlapped. Red and cyan, green and magenta, and blue and yellow are complementary colors of both light and printing and paint.

When red, yellow, and blue are overlapped, only red and black can be obtained. By overlapping cyan, magenta, and yellow, the additional colors of red, green, blue, and black can be obtained. The reason this occurs is because cyan, magenta, and yellow each absorb one of the red, green, and blue colors. Red, green, and blue each absorb two of the colors. Cyan overlapping yellow produces green; cyan overlapping magenta yields blue (Woolf, 1997).

The sun appears to be yellow because it is a combination of red plus green. The initial white light of the sun is separated by the atmosphere, which scatters the blue light and leaves the complementary color yellow as the color that we perceive as the sun. Because the blue component is scattered into the air, the eye perceives a blue sky. We see green grass because green absorbs red and blue light, which leaves only the green light for the eye to see (Shlain, 1991).

The rainbow includes primary and secondary colors. The order of colors in a rainbow as determined by decreasing wavelengths is red, orange, yellow, green, blue, indigo, and violet. This order can be remembered through mnemonics such as ROYGBIV or Richard of York gave battle in vain. Some scientists combine indigo and violet into one color and acknowledge only six distinct colors instead of seven.

According to Woolf (1997), human vision relies on light sensitive cells in the retina of the eye. There are two types of sensors in our eyes: rods and cones. Rods are cells that operate in low light intensity and cannot see color. Cones are cells that can see color, but require a much higher light level. The information from both the rods and the cones sends messages to the brain that allow us to see. Our eyes are sensitive to the three primary additive colors because they contain three different types of cones—red, green, and blue—and each cone allows us to see that color of light. Our brain interprets different amounts of red, green, and blue light that hit our eyes at once as various colors.

Our brains average the colors that strike our eye according to the order found in the colors of the rainbow. We observe yellow when equal amounts of red and green light meet our eyes because yellow is between red and green in the rainbow. If equal amounts of red, green, and blue light are detected, we actually see a white light. If we have no light, we see black.

New Approach to Intelligence

Information about the colors of the spectrum and different kinds of rainbows and colors made me realize that individuals actually process with primary, secondary, and complementary intelligences, creating a relationship that can be interconnected.

Our secondary intelligences are less dominant and not as bright. They also may be used in different ways.

The Chinese seven color spectrum prescribes that color is a manifestation of light and energy refracted in or through a prism. Light creates the sequence of colors in the rainbow (Rossbach and Yun, 1994). The Chinese view the rainbow as a symbol of nature's power and beauty. When light (energy) passes through a prism, only then can the colors of the rainbow be seen.

The following spatial model describes visually a new approach to intelligence.

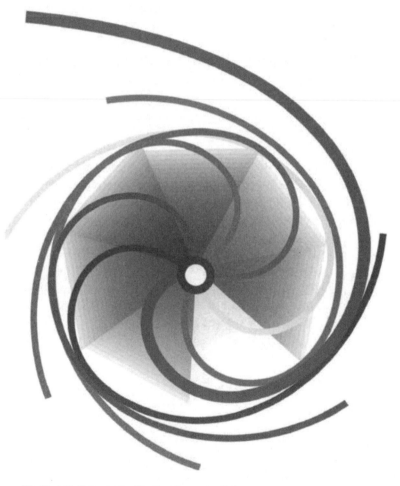

Each of the spirals in the model represent a color of the rainbow or one of the primary intelligences. There are gradations within each color. The seven colors spiral both in and out, signifying infinite possibilities for individuals to process information. The colors may represent neurons in the brain that spiral or branch out to reach new creative pathways. The gradations of color indicate the different strengths of each intelligence, which can vary depending on how the intelligence is used.

The mind is symbolized by the white light in the center of the spiral. It is like a bird's eye that can see things from different angles. The black circle around the white light represents the colors of printing and paint and completes the eye. We need both types of colors to perform different functions. The color white reflects all the colors. Without light, there is no color. The color black absorbs all the colors. Absorption requires a light source. Together the colors black and white are like the iris of an eye that pulls color both inside and outside. This iris radiates the blending of the seven colors, which complement each other.

Each individual perceives with different eyes. When we look at the center of the spirals they are moving inward and outward at the same time. This pull and tug represents life and continues throughout our lives. Even the shaded colors underneath do not stop spiraling. The more intense color is toward the center. As the colors spiral out they present a feeling of solidarity. Some of the colors or intelligences can overlap and work in tandem. It is possible that all of the intelligences intermingle at some time and place. They need to blend and harmonize with one another to perform different functions.

The center's core is very strong and signifies energy that can radiate and disperse to create new matter or intelligences. The core provides a balanced approach to learning. The spirals create the image of a pinwheel that is not pinned down or held back, but is able to propel itself forward, building velocity as it whirls outwardly. Individuals, like pinwheels, need to be allowed to propel themselves into creative and productive endeavors.

If the rainbow is formed using combinations of colors and if light provides energy when it passes through a prism, then this concept can be applied to multiple intelligences. The primary intelligences are linguistic, logical-mathematical, spatial, musical, bodily-kinesthetic, intrapersonal, and interpersonal. Because the naturalist intelligence appears to possess overlapping characteristics of several of the primary intelligences, it can be viewed as a secondary intelligence. Given that secondary colors are the combination of primary colors, the naturalist can be defined as possessing two or more primary intelligences blended into a combination of intelligences. This combination spirals out from the center to form a separate intelligence. By absorbing the colors or the strengths of the other intelligences, the naturalist intelligence acquires its own unique characteristics as it spirals past the other intelligences. It then creates its own identity and power!

Students often learn by combining two or more intelligences. Learning geometry requires logical-mathematical and spatial intelligences. Writing requires linguistic, bodily-kinesthetic, and intrapersonal intelligences. Playing the piano blends musical, linguistic, logical-mathematical, spatial, and bodily-kinesthetic intelligences and may additionally use both of the personal intelligences.

The colors in the rainbow and the combinations of the intelligences must be revealed in all students. Like the colors, the primary, secondary, and complementary intelligences overlap each other and can be blended together. If teachers teach using all of the intelligences, students will be able to see the total beauty of their "rainbow" of potential. One intelligence equates to one raindrop. Seven intelligences equate to the rainbow. There may be gradations of intelligences to consider. The primary intelligences may be dominant, but may need secondary intelligences to complement them. Intelligences can mix with other intelligences and create different ways for students to learn.

Gardner suggested that there may be additional intelligences to add to the list. Creating the series of spirals that blend with each other affords the opportunity to add or blend with what already exists.

Every individual has all of the colors in the rainbow or all of the intelligences, but those colors have different strengths and combinations that which make each person process information uniquely. If someone's intelligences are unable to spiral outward, then that individual is not allowed to use his or her talents or abilities to full potential. Too often individuals are held down and not encouraged to utilize their dominant intelligences in effective and successful ways. It takes all the intelligences, or colors of the rainbow, to create an individual's infinite capabilities. Teachers can provide the sunlight that assists students' colors to shine through each raindrop and combine to form the rainbow. The core of the spiral of colors is well balanced and strong. This provides a safe and secure area for growth and development. As the colors inter-mingle and build momentum, individuals are challenged to re-spond more creatively and advance to higher levels of thinking.

Our intelligences are similar to the metamorphosis of a cater-pillar into a butterfly. The butterfly begins as an egg, moves into a larval or caterpillar stage, and changes or molts its skin four or five times as it develops. It then forms a chrysalis. Although it does not move or eat, important changes occur inside the cocoon. When the adult is completely formed, it breaks the skin of the chrysalis and chews through the cocoon. Slowly the adult emerges and remains in the sun for several hours to allow its wings to dry (Julivert, 1991). Finally the butterfly is able to fly.

Individuals, like butterflies, undergo great changes in their developmental progression that are similar to a metamorphosis. Sometimes there is a hunger for learning and need to eat more from the fountain of knowledge to grow and develop. Learning progresses through different stages of development throughout one's life.

As individuals learn and grow in their developmental progres-sions, they gain confidence within themselves. Individuals are always changing through these developmental stages. Sometimes they become more like a cocoon and, although to the outside world nothing is happening, changes are occurring on the inside. This could be a time of intrapersonal reflections.

It is important in education to support students throughout the developmental process and all the changes that occur within it. Integrating multiple intelligences into the educational process allows greater opportunities for students to develop their creative potential because they are able to spread their wings and fly, and continue to grow and expand, rather than be held down by being allowed to demonstrate what they know in only one or two ways.

As society moves into the 21st century, it will increasingly become more important for the educational system to create many opportunities for students to develop their ability to think creatively, critically, and independently, to learn how to solve problems, to envision new ideas or products, and to be able to work both intrapersonally and interpersonally.

The model presented in this chapter demonstrates how to focus on the many different ways students learn. By providing a rainbow of opportunities for all students, all students can develop to their full potential. They can reveal their prism of colors when they are allowed to use the full spectrum of intelligences.

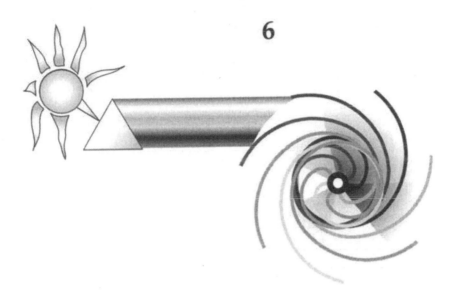

6

Conclusions

The National Commission on Teaching and America's Future Report (1996) recommended a restructuring of elementary and secondary education in two directions: to increase teachers' knowledge and skills to more effectively meet students' needs and to recognize and utilize teachers' expertise in schools that are redesigned to support and enhance high quality teaching and learning and to achieve their academic mission.

The report indicated that many high school students cannot read, write, compute, and solve problems with other people, do not possess technical skills, and are unable to manage scientific material at the high levels required for today's current workforce. Studies like the TIMSS report support this information.

I suggest another recommendation be added to this report: increase teachers' awareness of the different ways students process information and provide opportunities for them to design teaching methods that address the multiple dimensions of student learning. The relationship of intelligence to the learning process must be included in any discussion of ways to achieve higher academic achievement and student success.

Most schools have not produced the kinds of learning experiences required to allow our students to function productively in the 21st century because the current educational system does not support doing this. Teachers must know their subject area in depth, understand the many different ways students learn, and be able to design methods to create experiences that produce effective and long-term success in learning. The wide range in the learning needs of students today require educators to explore many different strategies to accommodate diverse student needs. Educators must continuously access current knowledge about how students learn and methods to effectively teach and assess these learners.

The discussion should focus on how to redesign schools to create environments for both students and teachers to experience success. There should be more time for both students and teachers to deepen their academic content knowledge, more personalized relationships between teachers and students, and greater opportunities for teachers to work and plan together in teams and to broaden collaborative partnerships with the community. To accomplish this will require reallocation of time, staffing, and perhaps even busing schedules. Collaborative teams can enable teachers to share their expertise, plan more effectively for student success, and use their time more productively.

The educational community cannot be an island unto itself, but must take into account wide societal perspectives and respond with appropriate action. There are no quick fixes, no "shot-in-the-arm" solutions to the problems that both society and education are facing today. These problems reflect each other. Everyone must become involved and come together to reach acceptable, long-lasting solutions (Fullan, 1991).

The theory of multiple intelligences offers an effective model for understanding how all individuals learn, regardless of gender, ethnicity, cultural background, or socioeconomic status. The intelligences often interact and work together to reinforce each other. Each individual possesses all of the intelligences, but in varying degrees, and certain intelligences sometimes dominate others. Educators should try to match each student's ability profile to a variety of different educational methods, rather than teach in only one or two ways and expect all students to understand. It has been established that students become actively engaged in learning when teaching methods are directed to one or more of their dominant intelligences.

Intelligence evolves through a dynamic of the individual's competencies and society's values and institutions (Gardner, 1996). We must look at the policies we are creating to support initiatives that effectively engage individuals' minds. We must question if the current initiatives accurately prepare our students to become active, participating members of an increasingly complex society. As we move quickly into the 21st century, neuroscientists are beginning to learn which neural structures are involved in which intellectual activities. Is this information being integrated into educational programs?

The ideal educational environment should draw upon students' love of learning and help them fully reach their potential. The ideal classroom should encourage high academic achievement of all students through interdisciplinary, relevant learning that builds on problem solving and in-depth understanding of content. Students must be provided with opportunities to learn how to interact with one another in a positive, collaborative manner, but also must have experiences that allow them to reflect and process independently.

Many current classrooms are directed only to the linguistic and logical-mathematical students, which leaves students who process information with the other intelligences to struggle because the information is presented in a format that they cannot readily understand or process. Through understanding multiple intelligences and identifying dominant intelligences, educators can develop increasingly effective teaching strategies to match learning with instruction. They can also develop multiple assessment measures that match those intelligences and teaching methods that accurately reflect what knowledge students have acquired. Applications of multiple intelligences and a variety of assessment measures provide a productive vehicle for creating a more engaging active learning environment.

Incorporating multiple intelligences into the classroom offers a strong indication that student achievement will increase, while students enjoy deepening their knowledge of academic content.

Significant evidence indicates that educators need to understand the effects of experiences on the development of the brain, the ability of the brain to utilize different pathways to learning, and the memory processes involved in encoding skills into long-term memory (Bransford, Brown, & Cocking, 1999).

Diamond (1988) stated that increasing the stimulus through environmental enrichment increases dendritic length and branching. Frequent new learning experiences and engaging mental challenges are critical for encouraging brain growth. Students need a multisensory environment that is engaging and relevant. The educational environment should create novelty and challenge. Learning is progressive. Students must be encouraged to explore and create new ideas. It is imperative that all students learn to read, write, and compute, but they must also learn to analyze critically, solve problems, and evaluate alternative solutions to problems.

Multiple Intelligences as a Philosophy of Education

Multiple intelligences should be viewed as a philosophy of education that provides a framework for examining individuals' differing strengths and developing the full spectrum of intelligence. This philosophy focuses on the content of learning and its relationship to different disciplines. The goals for education should be to want to teach content in ways students can understand, to prepare students to be able to succeed beyond the schooling environment, and to fully develop each student's potential. We need to say to students, "Your potential has no limits, except the ones you place on yourself."

Learning must become incorporated into everyday life experiences. There has to be a shift in teaching and learning from teacher-centered activities only to a blending with student-centered activities.

Teachers need to be able to reach each of their students through direct and effective methods. They must understand and possess the content knowledge to teach. Students must be introduced and exposed to innovative teaching and rich content, which requires a blending of implicit and constructivist teaching methods. Students need to be allowed to explore, take risks, be creative, and investigate ideas and possibilities. The emphasis cannot be only on right and wrong answers. Students must be encouraged to probe deeper to arrive at a more in-depth understanding of academic content knowledge. The focus cannot be only on results, but also on the methods for inputting knowledge. To prepare students for productive participation in society, meaningful learning experiences must be provided for all students.

It is not enough to read about content only, because students have to experience what they are reading to be able to engage the brain into long-term memory. When students research content knowledge and are then given creative opportunities to apply that research, they are elevated to much higher levels of processing information. It must be noted that when students are actively engaged in the learning process, discipline problems decline significantly.

It is important for teachers to present both theoretical and practical knowledge and to become more aware of individual differences and common traits that characterize children and adolescents during different developmental periods. The focus in teaching is not only to explore academic content knowledge through comprehension and applications, but also to analyze and evaluate students responses to problem solving and provide opportunities for them to create meaningful demonstrations of knowledge. This approach ensures long-term growth in both teaching and learning.

Vision for the Future of Education

The spatial model I presented in Chapter 5 is a dynamic, powerful, engaging interaction of all of the intelligences. The spirals in the model demonstrate the connections the different parts of the brain must make to perform various functions. In education, we need to gain a broader understanding of who we are and acknowledge that we may think and learn in very different ways. We must view both ourselves and others through new lenses, which requires a different, more open, and balanced approach to education.

I have followed closely the discussions of differing philosophies of how we should teach mathematics, science, and reading, and I offer some observations.

We must change the course of the discussions from arguing, bickering, and fighting, while holding on to each groups' conviction that there is only one way to view what is right and appropriate for the educational environment. We must, instead, attempt to work together for the sake of education, society, and our students' future—through a more collaborative process we can concentrate on developing new ideas and methods that take the best of all the different philosophies and focus on what will assist students in deepening their academic content knowledge, increasing their understanding of what they are learning.

It is agreed that both students and teachers require more in-depth content knowledge, but how that content is presented will make the difference in whether that learning is sustained or not. It must be presented in ways that allow students to understand why the content is relevant to their lives.

Armstrong (1994) stated, "The theory of multiple intelligences can serve as a template in constructing strategies for student success." When students become involved in the learning process and believe they are active participants, they will become more motivated and see the relevancy of why it is important to learn. The personalization of education occurs when connections to the content being learned are made to individual students' life experiences.

Learning is a complex process because students learn in many different ways. The possibilities for learning are as infinite as the combinations of colors in the spectrum of the rainbow. The rainbow is the symbol of nature's power and beauty. All the colors are blended and balanced to reflect the harmony of colors. Light is the source for the color sequence. When light, or energy, passes through a prism, only then can the richness of the colors be seen. Faceted crystal balls receive sunlight and transform the light into a rainbow of refracted color. They convey a positive, nurturing environment.

A prism is cut perfectly to reflect light. I suggest that the dispersion of the light of knowledge has to be spread throughout a different prism in the educational environment. A prism is a special form of geometry. It takes the light and disperses all the colors for others to see. Without the prism, only white light exists and that is invisible. We must find ways to allow all the colors in the prism to be dispersed in every classroom.

The spatial model (see page 78) signifies a new way to explore education. Out of the dark clouds comes a blue horizon that creates a new dawn. If we look at the human potential, it is infinite

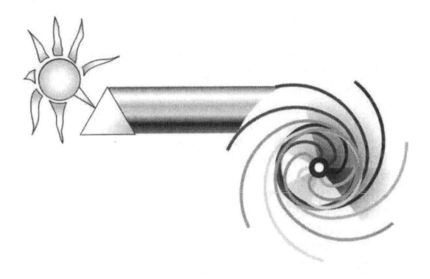

like the spirals that emanate from the center, or eye, of the circle. The sunlight creates energy for each student's potential and allows many colors to be dispersed from the educational prism that exists today. The center provides stability and focus. As the spirals move out from the center, they gather momentum as they pass through the different colors or intelligences.

One of the major problems in education has been the way the colors have been fed into the prism. Only one or two raindrops of color have been allowed to enter the educational environment. Because each raindrop represents only one color, this approach limited the reflection of learning for all students. As a result, a limited potential of students' ability or color has emanated from the prism of education. Many students have been unable to develop their full potential because their colors, or intelligences, have not been allowed to shine. We have restrained students or held them down like a pinwheel that is not allowed to propel itself forward and spiral out creatively. A critical change must be made in the educational process.

The goal of education should be to develop lifelong learning skills and a deep desire and joy for learning within all students. Student understanding and retention of information can increase when students are able to process information in ways that enable them to succeed and when the curriculum is taught with interactive and practical methods that allow students to tap into all of their intelligences.

Chapter 7 has been designed to provide practical applications of lessons that can be integrated into any curriculum area at various grade levels. The seven units have been created to act as starting points for teachers' creativity to spiral out into their own domains. I believe that, to model what I have written in this book, I had to create the units to demonstrate how to begin the process of extending the spectrum of learning to all students. I have combined academic content knowledge with practical methods for students to experience that knowledge. I have also included some general content standards that are appropriate for these units.

The vision for education as we enter the 21st century must be a resurgence of the thirst for knowledge, an eagerness and desire to learn, and greater opportunities for all students to engage in more in-depth learning activities.

We have the ability to provide an educational system that enables all students to achieve at their own pace, assures them positive means of reinforcement, and enables them to learn not only the basic skills, but more advanced content skills that can be translated into real life experiences. A supportive educational climate that provides for innovation, recognizes the uniqueness of all students, demonstrates the relationship between the brain and learning, provides for multiple measures of assessment, promotes excellence, and encourages high academic achievement for all students must be established in our schools to bring us successfully into the complex, technological new century. It is essential that students be engaged in rigorous academic content that requires them to think creatively and critically, to research information, and to develop into thoughtful, intellectual scholars. The learning environment must be redesigned to allow this to occur in every educational setting.

Einstein (Calaprice, 1996) said, "Wisdom is not a product of schooling, but of the life-long attempt to acquire it." Learning is a lifelong experience. Through a collaborative endeavor, members of the educational community can create a colorful prism for education that allows all students to develop their full spectrum of learning.

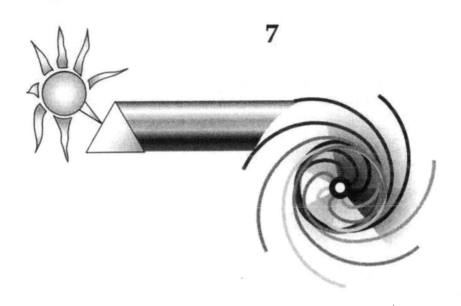

Classroom Units That Incorporate Color and Multiple Intelligences

As I was writing this book, I began to develop units on color that I thought might assist teachers as they integrate multiple intelligences into their classrooms. This chapter presents seven different units that can be used by teachers at any grade level. I have purposely not given specific grade levels for these units because I have found that most units can be adapted to different grade levels and teachers can make the appropriate adaptations.

I have field-tested most of these units with teachers who participate in the classes I teach at the University of California, Riverside. The units include objectives, activities to implement these objectives, identification of how the different intelligences are integrated into the activities, content areas discussed in the unit, applications of the state and national standards in language arts, reading, history, writing, social science, mathematics, and science, and several different assessment measures. The standards referenced are from the California content standards in science, history-social science, mathematics, and language arts (State of California Board of Education, 1997a, 1997b, 1998a, 1998b).

I have discovered that when teachers develop lessons that represent all or most of the intelligences, they are able to become more creative and design lessons that provide opportunities for all their students to become actively engaged in the learning process.

Unit 1

Primary, Secondary, and Complementary Colors

Objectives

- To have students understand the significance of color in their lives
- To understand the differences between the primary colors of light and the primary colors of printing and paint
- To understand measures of central tendency, estimation, and probability
- To develop graphing skills
- To use writing to express feelings and communicate expository information
- To demonstrate analytical thoughts and command of standard English
- To demonstrate aesthetic, poetic writing

Content Areas Included in This Unit
Language Arts, Mathematics, Science, and Art

Activities

Linguistic
- Have students write down their favorite color and state why.

Interpersonal
- Have students share with a partner why that color is their favorite.

Bodily-Kinesthetic
- Ask students to walk around the room individually and write down the different colors they see.

Spatial *Interpersonal*	• Determine the highest number of colors identified in the room. Give some type of award to the student who observes the most colors.
Linguistic *Interpersonal*	• Conduct individual surveys of at least 10 students in the room and ask each of them their favorite color.
Logical- *Mathematical* *Spatial*	• Chart and graph the findings of the surveys. Rank the colors from most popular to least popular. This activity can include an explanation of measures of central tendency (mean, median, and mode), how to use these measures to analyze findings in their surveys, and some statistics and mathematics skills such as estimation, and probability. Ask students to first estimate which two colors will be the most popular. What is the probability that these same two colors would be the most popular if 100 individuals were surveyed?
Linguistic *Interpersonal* *Logical-* *Mathematical*	• Ask the students to share with the class the mean, median, and mode for the results of their surveys and how they used estimation and graphing skills to interpret their findings.
Linguistic *Logical-* *Mathematical* *Musical* *Spatial* *Intrapersonal* *Interpersonal*	• Ask the students to write a cinquain about their favorite color. (A cinquain is a five-line poem that is arranged in a logical format and can include several of the intelligences.) Encourage students to draw a picture of their poem and present what they have written to the class. (Poetry encompasses musical intelligence because of rhythm and rhyme.)
Spatial	• Have each student draw a picture that describes the color in his or her cinquain.

Linguistic

• Explain to the students what the primary, secondary, and complementary colors are. Discuss the differences between the primary colors of light and the primary colors of printing and paint.

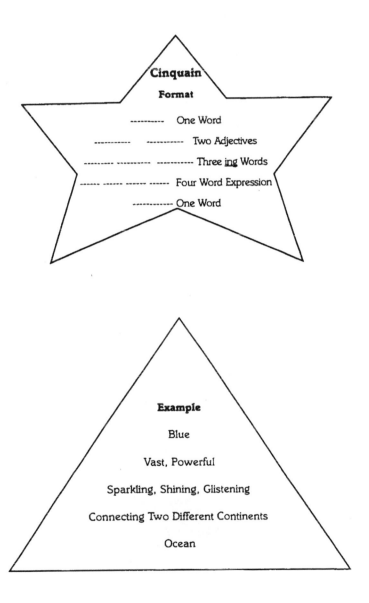

Cinquain

Format

---------- One Word

---------- ---------- Two Adjectives

-------- ---------- ---------- Three _ing_ Words

------ ------ ------ ------ Four Word Expression

---------- One Word

Example

Blue

Vast, Powerful

Sparkling, Shining, Glistening

Connecting Two Different Continents

Ocean

Linguistic
Spatial

- Explain to students that there are three primary colors of light (red, green, and blue) and three primary colors of printing and paint (magenta, yellow, and cyan). Show them the colors and have them make two triangles of colors as follows:

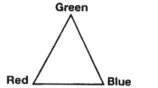 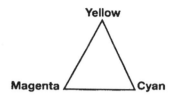

Logical-
Mathematical

- Discuss the differences between the types of primary colors and how we use them. Why do we need to use colors of light and when do we use colors of printing and paint? (Refer to Chapter 5 in this book for information on colors.)

Logical-
Mathematical
Spatial

- Chart how these two types of primary colors are alike and how they are different. Use a Venn diagram to illustrate the findings.

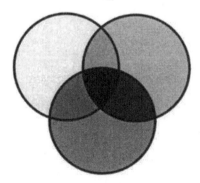

Spatial *Bodily-* *Kinesthetic* *Logical-* *Mathematical*	• Have students experiment with paints to mix colors together. Teachers who live in colder climates can let students mix different colors together in the snow. Have the students record their findings by writing or drawing descriptions of a sequence of steps they took and observations they made during their scientific investigation. Compare and contrast the results.
Bodily- *Kinesthetic* *Interpersonal*	• Ask the students to act out their favorite color for the class. Have the class guess the color.
Linguistic *Interpersonal*	• Share with students what different colors mean in our society, in schools, and in different cultures. (Information on how color influences our world follows this activities section on page 99.) Ask students to write their interpretations of how color is used in society and in schools. Have them share their drafts with two other students who conduct peer reviews of the paper and make both grammatical corrections and suggestions for editing and revising the drafts.
Musical *Intrapersonal* *Linguistic* *Spatial*	• Play the song "Colour My World" sung by either the group *Chicago* or Petula Clark or the song "Flowers are Red" by Harry Chapin. Have the students reflect on what colors the music reminds them of or let them draw their reflections as they listen to the music.
Linguistic *Musical* *Spatial* *Bodily-* *Kinesthetic* *Logical-* *Mathematical*	• At the elementary level, read *Brown Bear, Brown Bear, What Do You See?* (Martin, 1995) to the students. Purchase the bear puppet and bag of finger puppets described in the story or have students make their own puppets. Read the story and ask the students to chant the words, "Brown bear, brown bear, what do

you see?," and each successive set of words while other students pull the puppets, such as red bird, yellow duck, blue horse, green frog, out of the bag and hold them up as they are read. When the story is finished, ask the students to say which of the colors in the story are primary, secondary, and complementary. Which of the colors are part of the rainbow colors?

Linguistic
Musical
Intrapersonal
Interpersonal

• The students are to read the story again on their own or with a partner and identify the rhythm and rhyme patterns of the story. What is the theme or author's message in the book?

Spatial
Linguistic

• Ask the students to draw a picture of their favorite character in the book and write why it is their choice. Have them create their own book on colors using Martin's book (1995) as a guide.

Linguistic
Spatial
Interpersonal
Bodily-
Kinesthetic

• Read to the class *My Many Colored Days* (Seuss, 1996). Discuss the colors in the book and how the different colors make individuals feel. Act out the colors in the book by portraying what those colors represent. The students are to guess the color. What colors used in the book are primary, secondary, or complementary colors? Which colors can be seen in the rainbow?

Linguistic
Intrapersonal

• Ask the students to write how different colors create different feelings and emotions inside them. Do these emotions change? How? Explain what the word mood means. Can colors describe different moods or emotions? How?

Musical
Bodily-
Kinesthetic

• Analyze the rhythm and rhyme of the passages in the Dr. Seuss book. Have students clap to the rhythm.

Linguistic	• Read to students *Hailstones and Halibut Bones*
Interpersonal	(O'Neill, 1961) or do a choral reading with
Spatial	different students reading about each color.
Musical	Ask students to clap their hands as the poems
Bodily-	are read. Ask students which color they liked
Kinesthetic	best and why. Have them write their own
	"what is?" poem about their color. Draw a
	picture to describe the color. Read several
	poems in class.

Color Influences Our World

Color does influence our world. Color can affect our health, inspire emotion, influence our behavior, and determine what we wear and what we eat. In different cultures colors are symbolic. For example, in Western culture white is worn at weddings as a symbol of purity. In Chinese culture white is a symbol for death and burial and medicine. Green can represent vitality and symbolizes hope, spring, and growth. Red can symbolize justice and happiness and is often used at Chinese weddings. Yellow or gold provides a sense of tolerance, patience, and wisdom gained from past experiences. Blue or indigo has dual meanings. It can symbolize spring, new growth, and hope or it is a cold, mourning color. Blue–green is more aligned with nature and spring, the blue of the sky, and the green of bamboo and frogs. Brown symbolizes depth and the roots of wood. It creates a stable and established impression and reminds us of autumn.

Colors used in schools should not be dull or monotonous because they create a sense of boredom for students. All the brown furniture is too wooden, so the walls need to have more colorful, warm tones. Students need colors that make them feel comfortable. According to Rossbach and Yun (1994) colors such as green, blue, bluish-purple, and reddish-purple stimulate the brain and provide access to the students' energy.

Different colors create different environments. Brighter colors are needed to stimulate the brain and improve the students' mental and physical activities. Classrooms can mix color, using peaceful wall colors and off-white, and accents of livelier colors. Green is an effective color because it signifies new growth and possibilities. Red can provoke troubled students to become more anxious, and argumentative. Light green, pale blue, gray, and brown may calm unruly students. Yellow tends to highlight loyalty, honor, and truthfulness.

Assessments
Required Assessments for All Students

- Create a new color.
- Describe this new color.
- Write a composition on what meaning this new color has to society and personally.
- In a journal, assess what has been learned in this unit.
- Create an interpretative writing and/or draw something that expresses different emotions of color and how color influences every individual (this should be placed in the student's portfolio).
- Create a book on color that demonstrates the students understanding of primary, secondary, and complementary colors.

Students will be given a choice to complete two or more of the following assessments:

- Write a song about the two types of primary colors.
- Write a play about colors and perform the play.
- Write a poem about colors that demonstrates an understanding of primary, secondary, and complementary colors.
- Draw or paint a picture that signifies interpretations of color.
- Explain the applications of the colors of printing and paint and how and why they are different from the colors of light. Give examples.
- Chart and graph practical applications of color.
- Other measures of assessment that students discuss with the teacher

Standards

The *Mathematics Content Standards* covered in this unit include statistics, data analysis and probability, and mathematical reasoning with particular emphasis on measures of central tendency and methods for analyzing problems and finding solutions.

The *Language Arts Content Standards* that apply to this unit are in writing applications and their characteristics. Students are asked to write expository compositions that represent analytical thoughts to demonstrate their written work, support a command of standard English, and consider audience and purpose. The stages of the writing process from prewriting to drafting, revising, and editing successive versions should be demonstrated successfully. Students should write clear, organized, coherent, and focused sentences and paragraphs that elaborate a central overall theme.

The reading areas addressed in this unit are through the reading of stories, where students focus on comprehension and analysis, vocabulary development through color words, decoding, word recognition, and fluency.

The *Science Content Standards* covered in this unit include an investigation and experimentation strand. This strand is reflected in the experiment students conduct by mixing paints together. They are asked to sequence the steps involved in scientific investigations.

Unit 2

The Many Dimensions of Color

Objectives

- To study the importance of color and light in an Impressionist painting
- To interpret the meanings of different colors
- To understand primary, secondary, and complementary colors
- To compare the present with the past historical and cultural setting
- To apply map and global skills
- To identify both human and physical characteristics of a specific location
- To demonstrate the ability to research and write a composition

Content Areas Included in This Unit

Geography, History/Social Science, Language Arts, Mathematics, and Art

Activities

Spatial
- Find a book that displays the works of Paul Gauguin in color. Select his painting *Woman with Mango.*

Linguistic
- Discuss with the students information about Paul Gauguin's life (1848–1903). Emphasize that he was a French Impressionist artist who used colors to express emotions. Gauguin used bold, flat colors and shapes to show emotion. His paintings were colorful and had a marked effect on modern painting and decorative de-

sign as he moved into the post-Impressionist period. He studied with Vincent Van Gogh.

Gauguin left France in 1891 when he was 43-years-old and sailed to Tahiti in search of purity and innocence. He wanted to find an untouched civilization that possessed those qualities. He believed the people in Tahiti were untouched by corrupt civilizations and, therefore, were still pure. He was married and had five children.

Logical-
Mathematical

• Look up Tahiti on a map or globe. Trace the journey from France to Tahiti. How far is Tahiti from your school?

Logical-
Mathematical
Linguistic
Intrapersonal
Spatial

• Research what Tahiti was like in 1891 and compare that time period to the present. How are the two time periods alike and how are they different? Use a Venn diagram to describe the comparisons or write a narrative about the comparisons.

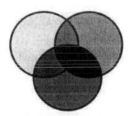

Linguistic
Interpersonal

• Using primary and secondary sources, research the historical period in which Gauguin lived. How did he influence culture through his paintings? Work in groups of two to four.

Linguistic
Intrapersonal

• Write a journal or diary of the trip Gauguin made from his point of view. Have students research the conditions of sailing during this historical period.

Spatial

• Look at the painting *Woman with Mango*. What do you think is the focus of the painting?
   - Where was the picture painted?
   - What clues assisted you? (Be sure to note the mango, flowers, and colors.)
   - Review what the primary colors of light are (red, green, and blue).

Linguistic
Spatial

• Review what the secondary colors are; that is, two or more primary colors blended together:

$$red + green = yellow,$$

$$red + blue = magenta,$$

$$blue + green = cyan.$$

Spatial

• The students are to create their own color wheel to demonstrate the different types of color. Explain what complementary colors are.

Logical-
Mathematical
Spatial

• How many colors did Gauguin use in his painting?
   - Are they hot or cool colors?
   - Are they vibrant or muted?
   - Are they strong or weak colors?
   - Are they primary or secondary colors?
   - Which colors are complementary?
   - Where is white used? Why? What could be the symbolism of white?
   - What do the colors yellow, blue, purple, and orange depict?
   - Are the shapes and lines hard or soft? Curved or straight?

Spatial *Linguistic*	• Describe in writing or drawing what types of shapes are hard and soft, curved and straight, and why.
Linguistic *Interpersonal*	• Brainstorm as a group to find words to describe the mood or emotions of the woman in the painting.
Linguistic *Interpersonal*	• Have the students each write a story as if they were the woman in the painting. Exchange papers and conduct a peer review to check for descriptive writing, organization, focus, grammar, and punctuation.
Spatial *Intrapersonal*	• Notice where Gauguin signed his painting. Ask the students where they would leave their signature on their paintings? Why?
Logical- *Mathematical*	• Compare this painting to other Impressionist paintings. How are they similar? How are they different?
Musical *Intrapersonal* *Linguistic* *Spatial*	• Listen to the *Hawaiian Chant, Hula and Music* by Folkways Records or any Polynesian music to depict the flavor of the Polynesian islands. Have students describe or draw the emotions the music signifies to them.
Musical *Interpersonal*	• Have students create a chant of their own that depicts life on a Polynesian island and share it with the class.
Bodily- *Kinesthetic*	• Create a dance that depicts activities on a Polynesian island.
Spatial *Bodily-* *Kinesthetic* *Interpersonal*	• Have the students stand up and move in flowing lines to describe the painting. Have them divide into groups to represent sections of the painting. Have the different groups portray the entire painting as a group.

Spatial   • Create drawings or paintings that depict life
                       in the Polynesian islands. Experiment with
                       colors similar to those Gauguin used.

Linguistic   • Describe in writing or draw how both the
Spatial   physical setting and the human characteristics
                       make the island so unique. Explain how these
                       features form the unique character of Tahiti.

Assessments

- Compare present day Tahiti to 1891 and present this
  comparison to the class using several of the intelligences.
- In a journal, reflect on what was learned in this unit.
- Write a composition or draw what it is about the physical
  setting and human characteristics that makes the island of
  Tahiti so unique.
- Write, draw, create a song or chant, or act out depictions of
  life in the Polynesian islands.
- Research Gauguin's life and compare two of his paintings
  from different periods of his life. Reference his use of color.

Standards

Unit 2 incorporates several of the standards that are outlined
in the *History/Social Science Content Standards* and demonstrates
intellectual reasoning, reflection, and research skills. This unit
includes chronological and spatial thinking that require students to
use map and global skills to determine the location of specific
places and to place key events and people of a historical era into a
chronological sequence within a spatial context.

Students will be asked to identify the human and physical
characteristics of the geographical location they are studying and
explain how these features form the unique character of the place.

Students will compare the present with the past historical and
cultural setting, evaluate the differences, and research evidence by
using primary and secondary sources.

This unit incorporates several of the *Language Arts Content Standards*, including using descriptive words when writing, displaying organization, focusing on creating a multiple paragraph composition, locating information in references and texts, and quoting information sources.

Students will demonstrate revising and evaluating writing and how to apply written and oral English language conventions in the written work that considers punctuation, capitalization, spelling, sentence structure, and grammar.

This unit includes the following standards from the *Mathematics Content Standards*: mathematical reasoning and estimation skills to verify the reasonableness of calculated results and generalizations of results obtained and strategies used to extend to a new problem situation.

Unit 3

The Rainbow—A Spectrum of Colors

Objectives

- To understand what a spectrum is
- To understand both the visible and the invisible colors of the rainbow
- To become aware of the scientific characteristics of the rainbow
- To understand the meaning of white light

Content Areas Included in This Unit

Language Arts, Reading and Writing, Science, and Art

Activities

Linguistic

- Review with students the seven colors in the spectrum.

Logical-
Mathematical
Spatial

- Discuss ways to remember the colors of the rainbow and their order (red, orange, yellow, green, blue, indigo, violet).

R	O	Y	G	B	I	V
e	r	e	r	l	n	i
d	a	l	e	u	d	o
	n	l	e	e	i	l
	g	o	n		g	e
	e	w			o	t
Red	Orange	Yellow	Green	Blue	Indigo	Violet

Linguistic
Logical-
Mathematical
Spatial
Interpersonal

- Ask the students to provide their own ideas for remembering the order of the colors of the rainbow and to share with each other.

Linguistic	• Discuss the visible and invisible colors of the rainbow.
Linguistic *Logical-* *Mathematical*	• Discuss ultraviolet and infrared light. How are they different? Where is their placement in the rainbow? (Light waves that are longer than red cannot be seen at all, but they can be felt as heat. These are called infrared or heat waves.)
Linguistic *Logical-* *Mathematical* *Spatial* *Interpersonal* *Bodily-* *Kinesthetic*	• Select 11 students in the class who would like to act out the play, "The Legend of the Colors of the Rainbow" (that appears at the end of this unit). Have the students make a sun, 42 and 40.6° signs, and signs on colored paper that represent each of the colors—red, orange, yellow, blue, green, indigo, and violet. Also make a sign for ultraviolet and infrared.
	• Have the students read and practice the play once or twice so they can portray the colors. Act out the play.
Linguistic *Spatial* *Intrapersonal*	• When the students finish the play, have them write or draw what they have learned.
Interpersonal	• Share what was written or drawn with a partner.
Linguistic	• Explain how to define white light.
Linguistic *Logical-* *Mathematical* *Spatial* *Interpersonal* *Bodily-* *Kinesthetic*	• Work in groups of 5 to 8 to make a prism. Place a mirror inside a plastic box filled with water. Put the box opposite a window that faces the sun. Tape a white sheet of paper on the wall where the colors can be seen. Move the box and adjust the mirror to enable students to see the colors in the spectrum on the wall.

Bodily-
Kinesthetic
Linguistic
Logical-
Mathematical
Spatial

- Ask students to move their fingers in the water and observe what happens to the colors. They should keep a scientific log of their investigation. Ask them to make white light. How did they accomplish this? Why was white light formed? (White light is a group of waves in the spectrum. It is a mixture of different colors. Each color has a different wavelength.)

Spatial
Bodily-
Kinesthetic
Logical-
Mathematical

- Make a color top. Cut out a circle from cardboard. Draw seven equal-sized sections and color them the seven visible colors of the rainbow. Put the colors in the order of the rainbow: red, orange, yellow, green, blue, indigo, and violet. Make a hole in the middle of the circle and stick a pencil through it with the point of the pencil pointing down. Spin the top. What color is seen when the top spins? Why is that color seen? What has happened to the other colors?

Linguistic *Logical-* *Mathematical* *Interpersonal*	• Explain to a partner what happens when the top spins and why. Record your findings in a journal.
Linguistic *Spatial* *Logical-* *Mathematical* *Interpersonal*	• Read to the students *The Rainbow Fish* (Pfister, 1992). Show them the pictures as the story is read. Discuss what it means to share something that is important to you. What form of mathematics did the fish use to give away its scales? Students are to share information with one another in groups of two to four.
Spatial *Bodily-* *Kinesthetic*	• Ask students to create their own rainbow fish out of a paper plate. Draw the color patterns on the plate. Paint them and put glitter on the fish.
Linguistic *Logical-* *Mathematical*	• Ask students to retell the story in their own words. How is the rainbow fish like a rainbow?
Linguistic	• Discuss what a simile and a metaphor are. Locate them in the story. How do they complement the words in the story?
Musical *Interpersonal*	• Play the song "The World Is a Rainbow." Ask the students to discuss with a partner what the words mean to them. How is the world like a rainbow?
Linguistic *Spatial*	• Write or draw the meaning of the song.
Bodily- *Kinesthetic*	• Act out the words to the music.

Linguistic   • Discuss with a partner how the words in the
Interpersonal   song apply to society today.

Assessments

- Work together with a partner to make a more sophisticated prism that explores white light and the spectrum. Create methods for analyzing the colors.
- Design an experiment to interpret how the colors are formed in the rainbow.
- Write a composition that explains how the world is like a rainbow.
- Include in a portfolio of work drawings and written composition completed in this unit.
- Through drawing, poetry, musical composition, a play, or a story, display knowledge of the spectrum, colors of the rainbow, prisms, and white light.
- Write a new version of the play "Legend of the Colors of the Rainbow" and provide new descriptions for each color.

Standards

The *Science Content Standards* included in this unit are investigation and experimentation, physical sciences focused on light and its source, physical principles of living systems, and the sequence of steps involved in scientific investigations that reflect making predictions based on patterns of observation.

The *Language Arts Content Standards* that apply to this unit are in writing applications and reading. Students are asked to write compositions that represent analytical thoughts to demonstrate their written work and support their understanding in standard English. Through the reading of stories, students focus on word analysis, fluency, vocabulary development, and reading comprehension and analysis. Students are asked to become familiar with poetic devices, such as similes and metaphors, presented in the readings. The students are also asked to demonstrate an ability to write clear, organized, coherent, and focused sentences and paragraphs that elaborate a central overall theme.

Legend of the Colors of the Rainbow

By Sue Teele, PhD

Select 11 students to perform in this play. The characters include the narrator, the sun, and the colors red, orange, yellow, blue, green, violet, indigo, ultraviolet, and infrared. The students need to make up signs that say 40°, 40.6°, and 42°. Students who are acting out a color should have a colored piece of construction paper that matches the color so they can hold it up when they speak. A sun should be made for the sun to hold up when speaking. Ask the students to read and study their parts and practice together once or twice before they perform for the members of the class.

NARRATOR: Once upon a time, the colors of the rainbow met to discuss what role each of them played in forming the spectrum of the rainbow. There were seven of them—red, orange, yellow, green, blue, indigo, and violet. Two other members—ultraviolet and infrared—were there also, but could not be seen. Each color described its contribution to the world. (As the colors read their parts, they should step out and hold up the color they represent.)

RED: I am the blood of life. I epitomize love from the red rose to the Christmas poinsettia to the carnation. I warn you of danger and I am a sign of bravery. I am one of the three primary colors of light. I am very important. I am always the outer part of the rainbow and can be seen at 42°. I have the longest wavelength and am bent the least.

ORANGE: I am the color of harvest and health and beautiful sunsets. My vitamins make you well. My vegetables and fruits give you extra energy. I am a combination of red and yellow. I need both of you (turns to Red and Yellow) to form me.

YELLOW: I am very important too. I represent the sun, the moon, and the stars. I bring joy and warmth to the world and make people happy and full of laughter. I am a sunflower and a daisy, and I welcome spring with a daffodil. I am the light that shines with brightness.

BLUE: Let me share with all of you who I am. I am the second of the primary colors of light. I am the sky and all the water in the world. I bring peace, calm, and tranquility to the world. When you look down from outer space at the Earth, you can see the vastness of my color. I can be seen at 40.6°.

GREEN: I am the third of the primary colors of light. I am the lush grass, trees, and leaves, and am most vibrant in the spring. I am the shamrock that brings good luck. I give hope to life because I represent spring and I return each year bringing youth, vitality, and renewal. I provide beauty and contrast to the other colors.

VIOLET: I am the inner part of the rainbow and the shortest visible wavelength. I am used for food and medicines. I am a lovely flower. I can be seen at 40°. I am bent the most of all the colors in the rainbow.

NARRATOR: Indigo was the last of the seven colors of the spectrum to speak and quietly reflected.

INDIGO: I am the color of silence, twilight, and the deepest waters. I bring inner peace and balance to life. Although I do not speak very much, I am always there for all of you.

NARRATOR: Ultraviolet and infrared comment together:

ULTRAVIOLET and INFRARED: Although no one can see us, we are very much a part of creating the rainbow.

ULTRAVIOLET: I come from the blue−violet end of the spectrum. I have a shorter wavelength, but I sure have a lot of energy.

INFRARED: I am adjacent to red. I have a longer wave length, but do not have as much energy as ultraviolet.

NARRATOR: You have convinced me that each of you is very important to our world, but I want to try an experiment. Will you all come together and join hands to form a circle? I am going to put the sun behind you at a 42° angle. (The Sun stands behind the group and holds up the 42° sign and the sun sign.)

SUN: I am behind you and give you the light you need. Be still. I want you to see the flash of lightning and hear the roar of thunder. (Make the sound of thunder and rain. The colors act afraid.)

(The Sun continues.) I am going to make it rain very hard. Do you hear the loud noise of the thunder? Do not be afraid. Gather closer and form a circle because you need each other. Please form the circle in the same way we see the rainbow: red, orange, yellow, green, blue, indigo, and violet. (The group forms a circle.) Every rainbow is a full circle, but not everyone can see the circle from the ground. They usually see a bow or an arc. Please change your circle to form an arc. (The colors form an arc in the order of the colors of the rainbow.)

(The Sun continues.) Ultraviolet, please stand next to violet and infrared, stand next to red. We want to take a snapshot in our brains so we will remember the correct order in which you are seen. Each one of you has been created for a special purpose in life. Each one of you is unique and possesses very special abilities, but you need to work together and respect each other. You see, when white light is split into wavelengths and mixed with rain, all of you will be separated and then come together in a very beautiful pattern called a spectrum. Each raindrop contributes only one of your colors. Red and yellow, please step out because you are higher raindrops in the sky. (Red and yellow step out.) Blue and green, please come forward because you are lower raindrops. (Blue and green step out, but not as far and they bend down below red and yellow.) I want you to know that you are all very important and without you, the rainbow could not be formed. Can you see now how each one of you is unique as a separate color, but how necessary it is for your uniqueness to contribute to the completeness of the rainbow? (All of the colors nod and say together, "Yes, we do.")

NARRATOR: Colors, what do you think?

RED: Wow, I did not know how much we need each other and I accept my position proudly in the rainbow.

BLUE and GREEN (together): We thought we were not as important because we were seen at a lower level in the sky. Now we know why and we are very pleased to accept our place.

YELLOW: This has been so much fun. It made me very happy.

ORANGE: I sure want to share more and be helpful to you other colors whenever I can.

VIOLET: I never realized why I was always on the inside. Now I feel so important and I want to assist all of you if I can.

INDIGO: I have always wished for each of us to believe in ourselves and find inner peace. Now I believe that can happen because we have learned how to value and appreciate each other. We are ready to provide a beacon of hope for all with our beautiful array of colors in the sky.

ULTRAVIOLET and INFRARED (together): We are pleased to be a part of the rainbow with all of the colors.

ALL (together): Let us all be sure we work with every rainstorm so we can provide a great glow of color across the sky wherever we go.

NARRATOR: The colors of the rainbow emerge because the sunlight has energized each one of you. All of you must work together to create such beauty. I believe this same message applies in our society. Be proud and be recognized for who you are. Discover the richness of each other and appreciate how we must all work together to create beauty and harmony in our world today. (The narrator pauses for a moment and then looks at all the colors and speaks to the audience.) This is the end of our play and we hope everyone has learned a lot about the rainbow and its meaning to us, and why all of the colors are so valuable. You have demonstrated how unique and yet important all of you are to make the rainbow so beautiful. So please, everyone take a bow, one by one like a fan, in the order of the rainbow so once again we can all appreciate your beauty.

THE END

Unit 4

Exploring the Rainforest

Objectives

- To understand geographical locations of rainforests in the world
- To explore plant and animal life that exist in the rainforest
- To discover rainbows of color in the rainforest
- To understand the four levels of the rainforest
- To understand how to solve mathematics problems
- To write a composition that reflects analytical thoughts
- To understand vocabulary words that describe the rainforest

Content Areas Included in the Unit

Language Arts, Geography, Mathematics, and Science

Activities

Linguistic
Logical-
Mathematical

- Share some facts with students about the rainforest such as the following:
  - Almost all rainforests lie between the Tropic of Cancer and the Tropic of Capricorn.
  - Two-thirds of the world's rainforests are tropical; the other third are tropical moist and temperate.
  - Over 40 different kinds of rainforests are located in South America, Africa, Australia, Asia, Central America, and North America.
  - Although tropical rainforests are found on only 6% of the Earth, over two-thirds of all the plants and animals in the world live in the rainforests.
  - In the last 100 years, over half of the world's rainforests have been destroyed.

Spatial	• On a map, find where rainforests are located in the world. Point out the continents.

Musical *Spatial* *Linguistic*	• Play the audio tape "Come on Into the Rainforest" (Nayer, 1993). One side is set to music; the other is a narrative. Play the musical side first. As the music plays, show the colored pictures in the book that accompanies the tape. Then play the narrative side of the tape.

Logical- *Mathematical*	• Ask the students to list facts about the rainforest they have learned from listening to the narrative and music.

Logical- *Mathematical* *Spatial*	• Ask students to identify on a map or globe the locations of the continents that have rainforests and to show where the rainforests might be located on each continent.

Logical- *Mathematical* *Interpersonal*	• Ask students to work in pairs and make lists of the birds, mammals, insects, and reptiles and amphibians they believe live in a rainforest (Cunningham, 1993; Hinshaw, 1997). Put the categories in the table below on the board. Provide one entry in each category as a starter. (Other examples are included in the lists to assist the teacher.)

Birds	Mammals	Insects	Reptiles and Amphibians
Toucans	Monkeys	Butterflies	Snakes
Parrots	Orangutan	Beetles	Lizards
Hummingbirds	Anteater	Ants	Frogs
Eagle	Bats	Centipedes	Turtles
Hornbill	Sloth	Spiders	Alligators
Quetzal	Leopard	Bees	Crocodiles

Linguistic *Interpersonal*	• When students complete their lists, ask them to work with a partner and put adjectives in front of the words that describe members in each of the groups they have listed.

Linguistic	• Discuss with students the four levels of the rainforest (Parker, 1997):
	- Floor
	- Understory
	- Canopy
	- Emergent level
Spatial	• Show students a picture that demonstrates the levels of the rainforest.
Spatial *Linguistic*	• Ask students to draw their own picture that shows all four levels of the rainforest. They are to label and describe the levels in their picture.
Linguistic *Logical– Mathematical*	• Introduce an "imagine that" section where several facts are stated. For example:

    - Imagine a place where the temperature changes very little each day and very little during the year. Where is that place?

                                Answer: The rainforest

    - Why does the temperature not change very much all year?

    - Imagine a location where you cannot see sunlight on the ground. Where is that place?

                                Answer: The rainforest

    - What blocks the sunlight?

    - Imagine a place where it rains almost every-day? Where is that place?

                                Answer: The rainforest

Mathematics Problems

Linguistic *Logical– Mathematical* *Interpersonal*	• Rainforests are the wettest areas of land in the world. Over 32 feet of rain may fall during one year. If it rains everyday, what is the average number of inches of rain per day in one year? Students are to explain to a partner how they figured out their answer.

Logical-
Mathematical
Spatial

- Imagine you are on a journey through the rainforest. On your travels you see 36 legs. What combinations of animals could you see whose legs total 36? Create a mathematics problem to find a solution. Draw a picture of your problem.

Linguistic
Logical-
Mathematical
Spatial

- You see four parrots in the rainforest. They found 21 juicy berries to eat. How many berries can each parrot eat if they share the berries equally? Draw and write how you solved this problem.

Colors in the Rainforest

Linguistic
Spatial

- The rainforest is rich with many colors: the lush green color of the forest; the blue birds; scarlet, gold, and blue macaws; emerald tree boas; mandrills with their red, blue, and white bottoms and red and white faces; orange-banded beetles; blue, orange, red-striped, bright pink, green, and brown frogs; red, green, blue, and yellow toucans; hornbills; quetzals; motmots; chameleons, who change colors to match their surroundings; and hummingbirds (Charlesworth, 1997).

Linguistic
Spatial
Interpersonal

• What is the dominant color in rainforests? Discuss with a partner why that color is so dominant.

Linguistic
Spatial

• Read to the students, *Welcome to the Green House* (Yolen, 1993). Identify all the colors and sounds described in the story—the animals, birds, insects, and reptiles and amphibians. What color is used in the book to describe the rainforest?

Linguistic
Spatial
Intrapersonal

• The students are to create their own color book on the rainforest. Each page should represent the rainbows of colors found in the rainforest. Draw and write about the colors and species found in the rainforest.

Interpersonal

• Work in groups to answer the following question: What do we discover in the rainforest when we

Feel?	Taste?
Smell?	See?
Hear?	

Bodily-
Kinesthetic
Logical-
Mathematical

• Act out each of these senses in a pantomime. Have students guess which sense.

Linguistic

• Discuss what some of the products found in the rainforest are. For example, nuts, fruits, ingredients for medicine, hardwoods such as teak, mahogany, and ebony, tea, coffee, cocoa, rubber, and synthetic and raw materials used for food, clothes, tools, and cosmetics. Ask the students to conduct some outside research both on the Internet and with primary and secondary sources to complete this information.

Bodily-
Kinesthetic
Logical-
Mathematical
Spatial

• Demonstrate to students what a rainstick sounds like. Have them make their own rainstick, as follows:

- Take an empty paper towel roll. Tape it with clear tape on the end. Put 1/2 cup of rice and lentils in the paper towel roll. Seal it shut and paint, decorate, or use papermache on the outside of the rainstick.

Musical
Linguistic

• When all the students have made their rainsticks, play a symphony of different rainsticks. Have students write down what they think they hear while they are listening to the sounds.

Musical
Linguistic

• Listen to the song "Rainforest Rap." Discuss what the words "devastation" and "deforestation" mean.

Interpersonal
Linguistic
Musical

• Ask the students how they can save the rainforests. In groups of two to four write a verse for a song that discusses the rainforest. Combine the verses and have the class sing the song.

Linguistic
Intrapersonal

• Read the *Great Kapok Tree* (Cherry, 1990). Discuss how the animals convinced the lumberman not to chop down the kapok tree. Select an animal from the story and write a story as if you were that animal.

Logical-
Mathematical

• Discuss the water cycle.
  - It falls as rain
  - The rain is absorbed by trees and vegetation.

- It is passed into air as water vapor during photosynthesis.
- It evaporates in the sun from rivers, streams, pools, and lakes.
- Water vapor forms clouds.
- Water then falls again as rain.

Logical-
Mathematical
Spatial

• How does the water cycle work in a rain-forest?
• Have students draw the water cycle process and label the stages of the process.

Linguistic

• Ask students to define vocabulary words that are found in a rainforest and learn how to spell these words.

climate	ecosystems	habitat
photosynthesis	evaporate	camouflage
foliage	water vapor	emergent
lichen	epiphytes	extinction
slash-and-burn		

Spatial
Linguistic

• Students are to draw a picture of something that represents for them each of these words. They are then to write that word, spelled correctly, several times within their picture. Tell them that when they hear the word, they should try to envision the picture and the correctly spelled word inside. Then give them a spelling test and see how well they do. Allow them to draw their pictures when taking the test if that will assist them.

Linguistic
Interpersonal
Logical-
Mathematical

• Read aloud "The Cowrie Thieves" from *Life in the Rainforest* (Baker, 1990), which is a story about a village in the Congo in Africa. Discuss with a partner the theme of the story. What is the meaning of this story? Compare this story to a situation today. Write a composition on a similar modern-day story.

Assessments

- The students are to select a composition they have written that represents first draft to finished product and a drawing they have done, and place them in their portfolio.
- Students are to select two of the following measures of assessment:
  - Write a song or play that contains information learned about the rainforest.
  - Design a pop-up book that demonstrates content about the rainforest.
  - Write a cinquain that describes the rainforest and draw a picture to depict the poem.
  - Create an examination that will assess the students' knowledge of the content covered in this unit. Give the test to other students in the class. Grade the examination and provide notes for classmates about what they could have included on their examination that would have demonstrated their understanding of the information.
- Ask every member of the class to make a unique and original contribution to the classroom that will assist in creating a rainforest environment in the entire classroom. Each student will be credited in their assessments for their contributions.

Standards

The *Mathematics Content Standards* included in this unit are problem solving, number sense, mathematical reasoning, and computation skills.

The *History/Social Science Content Standards* reflected in this unit include chronological and spatial thinking that require students to use map and global skills to determine the location of specific places. Students are asked to identify the human and physical characteristics of the rainforest and to explain how these features form the unique character of the place.

The *Science Content Standards* that are included in this unit are investigation and experimentation, physical science that includes the physical properties of substances that can change, and life sciences that reflect different plants and animals, habitats, and environments.

The *Language Arts Content Standards* that apply to this unit are in writing applications and reading. Students are asked to write compositions that represent analytical thought and demonstrate their understanding of standard English. Through the reading of stories and listening to songs, they can focus on word analysis, fluency, vocabulary development, spelling, and reading comprehension and analysis. The students are asked to demonstrate their ability to write clear, organized, coherent, and focused sentences and paragraphs that elaborate a central overall theme.

Unit 5

Pandas—Endangered Species

Objectives

- To gain a better understanding of giant pandas and how they live
- To identify meaning associated with the colors of the pandas and society
- To apply map and global skills
- To develop skills in solving mathematics problems
- To demonstrate the ability to write a composition that communicates analytical thoughts and command of standard English

Content Areas Included in This Unit
Language Arts, Geography, Mathematics, and Science

Activities

Linguistic
- Provide an introduction to this unit with information about the giant pandas. Giant pandas are an endangered species. It is believed that there are less than 1,000 pandas left in the wild and 100 in captivity. Giant pandas can be found in the mountains of China above 6,000 feet. They cannot survive very long if the temperature goes above 75° (Petty, 1992).

Mathematics Problem 1

*Logical-
Mathematical
Interpersonal*
- Work with a partner to figure out the following problem. If there are approximately 1,000 pandas left in the wild and pandas live for 25 years, can mate from about 4 to 10 years, and have a baby panda every 2 years, estimate how many pandas there will be in 25 years.

Spatial

• On a map or globe, locate where China is. Years ago pandas also lived in Laos and Vietnam. Locate these three countries on the map. Draw a map of China. Is it a large or small country? How far away is China from your school?

Linguistic
Spatial

• The panda is a symbol of China. What is the symbol of the United States? Guide students to understand what the bald eagle means in the United States.

Linguistic
Musical

• The Chinese name for giant panda is daxiong mao, pronounced dah-shwing ma-hoo (Feeney, 1997). Ask the students to pronounce the Chinese name for pandas and try to rhyme the name with English words so they can develop an association to the pronunciation.

Mathematics Problem 2

Linguistic

• Pandas grow to be about five feet tall and weigh between 200 and 350 pounds.

Logical-
Mathematical

• If it takes about 50 pandas to weigh as much as 1 elephant, figure approximately what an elephant weighs. Give a range based on the average weight of the panda.

Mathematics Problem 3

Linguistic

• Pandas spend up to 14 hours a day just eating. Almost all of their diet, close to 99%, is bamboo, but they can eat fruit, roots, wildflowers, fish, birds, and eggs (Feeney, 1997).

Logical-
Mathematical
Interpersonal

- A panda eats about 25,000 pounds of bamboo in 1 year. How many pounds is that per day? How many pounds of bamboo does a panda eat every hour? Ask students to explain to another student how they arrived at their solution and share the mathematical computations.

Linguistic
Spatial
Bodily-
Kinesthetic

- Imagine what life would be like if everyone ate food 14 hours a day. Write, draw, or act out how that would change daily activities. How would life be different?

Linguistic
Spatial

- Ask the students to draw what they think a giant panda looks like. Have them provide as much detail as possible. Have them write a descriptive paragraph that explains the panda's appearance.

Linguistic
Spatial

- Provide a detailed description of the giant panda after the students have drawn what they think it looks like and ask them to change their drawing and paragraph as they listen to the following description of the panda.

  The giant panda has a white face with black patches around dark brown eyes. The panda has a black nose, black ears that wiggle when it chews bamboo, white whiskers, and a pink tongue. The panda's fur is thick and assists in conserving heat and energy. The fur is also rough and bristly like a brush. The panda does not hibernate. Pandas clean themselves by rolling in dirt and using their claws to comb out the dirt. Then they lick their fur clean. Under the white fur is pink skin and under the black fur is dark skin (Feeney, 1997). Show students a picture of a panda and have them add what they see to their descriptions and pictures.

Logical-Mathematical	• Ask students why pandas have a black and white color combination? Why is the skin underneath the white fur pink and the skin underneath the black fur dark?
Logical-Mathematical	• Ask students to compare the panda's approach to cleanliness with their own. Which is better or more efficient? Why or why not?
Linguistic	• Ask students to add to their descriptions and drawings about the panda after they hear the following information.
	- The pandas have five fingers on each of their front paws and a special thumb that allows them to grab and hold bamboo. The pads of their paws are covered with fur that act as snow shoes for their feet. They have short, strong legs and stubby white tails. They walk somewhat pigeon-toed, with their front feet pointed inward. Pandas can swim, climb, and run like horses. The giant panda is near-sighted, but has a keen sense of hearing and smell (Feeney, 1997).
Linguistic *Musical* *Bodily-Kinesthetic*	• The pandas create silent messages for other pandas by clawing the trunks of trees. They carve out their own dominant territory that way. Pandas bark like dogs when in danger,

squeal like pigs when afraid, and roar like bears when mating (Feeney, 1997). Act out an imitation of pandas making a sound. The students are to guess if the sound is one of danger, fear, or mating.

Linguistic

• Pandas are shy, quiet, and solitary. They live together only when they are ready to mate or raise a cub.

Linguistic
Spatial
Intrapersonal
Interpersonal

• Ask students to draw and write what they now know about pandas. When they have completed the assignment, ask them to share their work with a partner and compare information.

Linguistic

• Discuss with students that pandas may not be bears at all, but may be more like the raccoon family.

Logical-
Mathematical
Spatial
Intrapersonal
Interpersonal

• Chart a comparison of the panda to the bear family. Make one chart of how they are alike and another on how they are different. Ask students to work alone at first and then compare information with a partner. (Provide one or two comparisons, but have students research the rest. I have provided some information for the teacher. Add to the lists.)

Alike

Pandas	Bear Family
Round heads	Round heads
Fat bodies .	Fat bodies
Thick fur	Thick fur
42 teeth	42 teeth
Lumbering gait	Lumbering gait
Climb well	Climb well
Agile in trees	Agile in trees
Mammal	Mammal

Different

Pandas	Bear Family
Do not hibernate	Hibernate
Back molar teeth wide and very large to crush bamboo	All teeth are large
99% of diet is bamboo	Eat a variety of fish, fruit, insects, roots, and small animals
Five fingers on front paw and special thumb to hold bamboo	Powerful claws for digging
Create silent messages by clawing on bark	Do not create messages on bark
Always black and white	A variety of colors, depending on the species
Live alone unless mating	Stay together as a family
Weigh between 200 and 350 pounds and stand 6 feet tall	Can weigh up to 1,200 pounds and stand 9 feet tall

Pandas are a mixture of raccoon and bear family.

Logical-
Mathematical
Spatial

- Examine the characteristics of the red panda and compare the red panda to the black and white panda. Create a Venn diagram to clarify how they are alike and how they are different. Ask students to decide which family they think the pandas should belong to if they could be a part of only one family, the bear family or the raccoon family. They are to support their decision with facts.

Linguistic	• Pandas can mate after they are 4 years old. They mate in the spring and have a 5-month gestation period. In the fall, a cub is born. The cub weighs only 4 ounces at birth and can fit into the palm of a hand. At 4 weeks of age, the cub is 10 times its birth weight.
Logical-Mathematical Interpersonal	• Ask the students to calculate how much the cub actually weighs at 1 month of age. A 1-year-old cub weighs around 70 pounds. Calculate how much weight the cub gains per month. The students are to share their answer with a partner and explain how they figured out the solution.
Logical-Mathematical	• Compare a panda cub to a newborn baby. Which grows more in weight from newborn to adult. Explain the answer.
Linguistic	• When a panda cub cries, it sounds like a baby. The cub is pink with all white fur when first born. When the cub is 1 month old it begins to develop black and white markings. It does not open its eyes until about 2 months of age.
Linguistic	• Pandas often give birth to twins. The mother will nurse up to 14 hours a day, about the same amount of time they eat as adults. When the mother leaves the den to find food for herself, she holds the cub to her chest with one paw and walks on three legs. Later the mother carries the baby with her mouth.
Spatial Linguistic	• Show a short segment of the video *Secrets of the Wild Panda* by National Geographic Video (1994) that films a live seven-week-old panda cub. Ask the students to share their reactions after viewing the video.

Linguistic   • Read the book *I Am A Little Panda* (Crozat, 1993) or *Big Panda, Little Panda* (Stimson, 1993). Discuss the story.

Linguistic   • Ask the students to write a cinquain about the
Logical-   panda in the book and draw a picture that
Mathematical   describes their cinquain. An example of one
Intrapersonal   follows:
Spatial
Musical

Pandas

Shy, Solitary

Eating, Sleeping, Playing

They Are Becoming Extinct

Preserve.

Bodily-   • Pandas like to play, tumble, and roll around.
Kinesthetic   They like to entertain themselves. Ask stu-
Interpersonal   dents to work in a group that represents two
                              cubs and a mother and to act out how the
                              pandas might play.

Linguistic   • Pandas are becoming extinct because hu-
Logical-   mankind is destroying the bamboo forests.
Mathematical   What does the word "extinct" mean? How
                              can the pandas be saved from extinction?
                              What other species are endangered? Why?

Linguistic *Intrapersonal* *Interpersonal*	• Discuss with students the symbolism of the panda in society today. Pandas can be considered as multicultural animals that represent several different cultures because they are black and white, have brown paws, and come from Asia. What can be learned about society by studying pandas?

Assessments

- All students should place in their portfolio or record of achievement two to three of the assignments they have completed for this unit.
- Students are to select two of the following assessments:
  - Write a composition that compares the plight of the pandas to problems in society today.
  - Create an examination that will assess what the class has learned from studying about pandas. Give the examination to the entire class and grade it. Provide critiques for other students regarding how they demonstrated their knowledge and understanding.
  - Write a play, poem, song, or book that demonstrates knowledge about pandas.
  - Create a mathematics problem for the class to solve that involves information about pandas.
  - Make a chart that compares the pandas with the raccoon family. Cite how they are alike and how they are different.

Standards

The *Mathematics Content Standards* included in this unit are mathematical reasoning, estimation skills to verify the reasonableness of calculated results, mathematical computation skills, number sense, and problem-solving skills.

The *Language Arts Content Standards* that apply to this unit are using descriptive words in writing, displaying organization, and focusing on creating a multiple paragraph composition that represents analytical thought. Through the reading of the story and writing assignments, students can focus on word analysis, fluency, vocabulary development, spelling, and reading comprehension.

The *Science Content Standards* that are included in this unit are life sciences with a focus on animals, habitat, and environment, and investigation and experimentation.

The *History/Social Science Content Standards* covered in this unit include chronological and spatial thinking that require students to use map and global skills to determine the location of specific places.

Unit 6

Butterflies and Moths—Colorful Insects

Objectives

- To understand similarities and differences between butterflies and moths
- To understand the stages in the metamorphosis process
- To develop graphing skills
- To use writing to express feeling and to communicate expository information
- To demonstrate aesthetic, poetic writing

Content Areas Included in This Unit

Language Arts, Mathematics, Science, and History/Social Science

Activities

Linguistic
Musical

- *Introduction*

- Butterflies and moths are insects that are members of the Lepidoptera order. Ask students to clap their hands as the teacher says the syllables of the word "Lepidoptera." Lepidoptera means scaled wings. The scales on the wings and bodies provide color. The scales rub off like powder (San Diego Zoo, 1995).

Linguistic

- There are more than 140,000 species of Lepidoptera in the world. They come in many different colors, sizes, and shapes (Julivert, 1991). Butterflies need to be warm to fly and do so by spreading their wings toward the sun. Moths, because they fly at night and do not have the sun to warm their wings, shake themselves to become warm. Butterflies and moths have three sections to their anatomy:

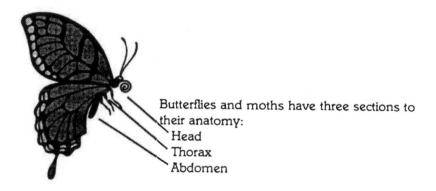

Butterflies and moths have three sections to their anatomy:
Head
Thorax
Abdomen

Logical-
Mathematical
Spatial

- Ask the students to research what the function of each section is. Show the students a model of an insect to demonstrate the three sections. Ask them to draw an insect and label the three sections. They should add to their drawing as the discussion continues.

Linguistic	• Discuss how the head is the sense organ where the antenna, compound eyes, and proboscis are located. Introduce the concept of compound eyes and how these eyes have facets that detect invisible ultraviolet light. Each facet is like a screen and each one works separately (Kalman and Everts, 1994).
Linguistic	• The proboscis is like a long tongue that allows the butterfly to probe deeply into flowers to reach nectar. The proboscis is coiled up underneath the butterfly's head when not in use (Arnosky, 1996).
Bodily-Kinesthetic *Linguistic* *Interpersonal*	• Have students experience what it is like to drink nectar with a proboscis. Fill a glass with water or juice. Connect three or four straws together to make one long straw. Put one end in the water and suck from the other end. Discuss the students' responses to this way of drinking.
Spatial	• The students are to add to their drawing a proboscis, antenna (which assists the insect in detecting odors), and compound eyes.
Spatial	• The thorax is the middle sections of the insect and it houses six legs and two large pairs of wings. The students are to draw the legs and wings on their insect.
Linguistic *Spatial*	• The third section is the abdomen. This is the largest section of the body and it houses the reproductive organs. The abdomen has spiracles or holes that let in air and allow the insect to breathe. The students are to add spiracles to the abdomen section of their drawing.

Linguistic

- Butterflies have an exoskeleton, which is a skeleton on the outside of the body that protects the soft insides.

How Are Butterflies and Moths Alike?

Linguistic
Logical-
Mathematical

- Both are caterpillars when they are young
- Both adults drink nectar from flowers through a proboscis
- Both have wings covered with tiny scales that come off easily if touched (they are the only insects that have scales)
- Most die when the weather gets cold
- Both have three sections—head, thorax, and abdomen

How Are Butterflies and Moths Different?

Linguistic
Logical-
Mathematical

Butterflies	Moths
Long antenna with a knob at the tip	Antenna comes in many sizes and shapes—some feathered and fringed
Bring their wings up over their bodies when resting	Fold their wings close to their bodies when resting
Usually large and colorful	Usually smaller and less colorful
Fly during the day	Fly at night
Thinner bodies	Fatter bodies

Bodily-
Kinesthetic

- The students are to make hand puppets of both a moth and a butterfly. Trace the shapes of a butterfly and a moth and have students cut out and glue them to tagboard or construction paper. Color both insects with crayons or colored markers and glue them to popsicle sticks.

Logical-
Mathematical
Bodily-
Kinesthetic
Linguistic
Interpersonal

• Using their puppets, the students are to write and present to the class a short play that presents information on how moths and butterflies are alike and different.

Vocabulary and Spelling Words

camouflage	exoskeleton
metamorphosis	proboscis
caterpillar	spiracles
head	pheromones
thorax	antenna
larva	abdomen
pupa	mimicry
cocoon	chrysalis

Linguistic
Spatial

• Discuss what each word means. Ask students to draw a picture of what each of the words means. Write the word several times within their picture. Give a spelling and vocabulary test, but allow the students to show what they know with more than one intelligence.

How Butterflies and Moths Use Colors

Linguistic

• Insects use colors to protect themselves and to act as warning signs (Legg, 1997).
  - Peacock butterflies have large colorful eye spots on their wings.
  - Owl butterflies look like leaves with their wings folded and have staring eyes when

their wings are spread open. They look like they are blinking.

- The Indian leaf butterfly is colorful when open, but looks like a leaf on a tree when closed.
- The monarch butterfly emits a bad smelling colored liquid when threatened.
- The caterpillar of a cabbage butterfly sends out a green substance when bothered.
- Some caterpillars have bright colors on their abdomens that warn enemies not to touch or small eye spots on their skin that makes them look like small snakes.
- Some butterflies and moths resemble poisonous ones and yet are not. This is called mimicry. They look alike, but one is harmless and the other is poisonous.

Bodily-
Kinesthetic
Spatial
Linguistic

• Students are to make their own butterfly and color it with colors that will protect it. Explain how the colors act as a sign of alarm.

Metamorphosis in Butterflies and Moths

Linguistic

• Butterflies and moths begin their lives as caterpillars. They go through four stages as they change.

• Read the book, *The Very Hungry Caterpillar* (Carle, 1987). Discuss what happened to the caterpillar. If given permission, show the video of the story, *The Very Hungry Caterpillar and Other Stories* by Walt Disney Home Video (1993).

Linguistic
Spatial

• Show the 5-minute video *See How They Grow —Insects and Spiders* from Sony Wonder (1994).

Linguistic

- Discuss the four stages of metamorphosis (Julivert, 1991; San Diego Zoo, 1995).

- 1. **Egg**. The male and female court each other. The female releases a pheromone, which is a fragrant substance that attracts males. The males' antennae pick up the scent of the female. The female lays hundreds of small creamy white eggs. (Monarch butterflies lay eggs only on milkweed plants.)

Linguistic

- 2. **Larva**. In 3 to 6 days a tiny white caterpillar chews its way out of the top of the egg and eats the shell. About 6 hours later, it develops stripes and begins to grow. Caterpillars eat as much as 20 times their weight in food. They must shed their skin several times to make room for bigger bodies.

Logical-
Mathematical

- *Mathematics Problem*. Ask students to figure out how much they would weigh if they weighed 3,000 times their birth weight in the first 15 to 20 days of their life.

Bodily-
Kinesthetic
Spatial
Logical-
Mathematical

- *Making a Caterpillar*. Take a one dozen size egg carton and cut the bottom in half lengthwise. Place the rims of the two halves together to create 6 compartments. Use tape to hold the halves together. Take a small paper plate or a piece of tagboard, trace a circle on it, and cut out the circle. The circle represents the head. Ask students to color the head and put 12 small eyes, 6 on each side, and antennae on the head. They can use 6-inch pieces of pipe cleaner for two antennae for both the front and the rear of the caterpillar. They can also use pipe cleaners to make 10 prolegs (which help the caterpillar crawl), 5 on each side, and 6 real legs, 3 on each side. Point out the head, the thorax, and the abdomen. Put small holes along the sides of the caterpillar's body for the spiracles, which allow the caterpillar to breathe. (Another way to make the caterpillar is to use small 1-inch pom poms and a styrofoam ball for a head.)

Linguistic

- 3. **Pupa.** When the larva finds the right spot, it begins to turn its head back and forth to attach silk thread that is called a silk button. It uses hooks on its last prolegs to hold the silk. Once the silk button is made, the caterpillar moves its body around and hangs from the silk button, forming a shape like a capital J. The transformation to a butterfly now begins. The caterpillar has to wiggle out of its skin. Its new skin hardens right away to form a chrysalis. Inside the chrysalis the eyes, legs, and body become a thick liquid. The body does not move. The pupa is smooth and green in color. Little pearls that look like gold begin to show in a groove. The word "chrysalis" comes from the Greek word *chrysos* which means gold. In 1 to 3 days the outer skin begins to turn clear. From days 4 to 8, the wings inside begin to unfold. From days 9 to 11, the colors of the butterfly form. From days

12 to 14, the wings and chrysalis become clearer. About an hour before the butterfly emerges, it releases a murky liquid that enables it to free itself from the walls of the chrysalis (Rosenblatt, 1998).

(*Note:* The moth weaves a cocoon and the chrysalis forms inside it, whereas the butterfly forms a chrysalis that hangs from a branch.)

Bodily-Kinesthetic
Spatial

- To have students understand what a chrysalis is, bring in green grapes that have the stems on them. Ask them to tie the grapes to a mobile and paint gold dots on them.

Linguistic

- 4. **Adult**. The adult butterfly begins to emerge from the chrysalis. It pumps fluids from its abdomen to its head and upper body to split open the chrysalis. It crawls out with its legs first and then turns around to hold on to the chrysalis. The wings hang downward. Once the butterfly is outside the chrysalis, it begins to pump fluid from its body to its wings to inflate them. The fluids have to move quickly because the wings harden if they do not receive fluid. It takes about 2 hours for the wings to dry and harden into their correct shape. When the butterfly is ready to fly, it tests its wings by opening and closing them to ensure they are dry. It is ready to fly and look for nectar. Then the cycle of life begins again (Rosenblatt, 1998).

Logical-
Mathematical
Bodily-
Kinesthetic
Interpersonal

• Ask students to enact the process of the butterfly emerging from the chrysalis. Work in small groups to be sure all the steps are followed.

Spatial
Logical-
Mathematical

• Students are to draw the entire process of metamorphosis. Label what happens during each stage.

Linguistic
Logical-
Mathematical
Spatial

• Ask students to write 12 to 14 sentences regarding what they have learned about moths and butterflies. Draw a caterpillar and place the sentences by strips into each of the segments of the caterpillar.

Linguistic
Logical-
Mathematical
Spatial

• Students are to draw a diamond on a sheet of paper. They will be writing a diamante, a seven-line poem in the shape of a diamond. This poem provides an opportunity for a grammar lesson because lines 1, 4, and 7 are nouns, lines 2 and 6 are adjectives, and lines 3 and 5 are action verbs.

Diamante

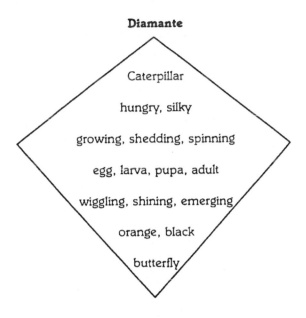

Caterpillar

hungry, silky

growing, shedding, spinning

egg, larva, pupa, adult

wiggling, shining, emerging

orange, black

butterfly

Spatial

• Students are to draw a picture to describe what they wrote in their poem.

Monarch Butterflies

Linguistic

• Monarch butterflies are unique because they migrate thousands of miles each year, some up to 2,500 miles. Explain to students what migration means. Monarchs cannot live where temperatures fall below freezing, so they have

to migrate to stay alive. Sometimes they ride
on wind currents, storms, and even hurri-
canes as they head to the south. The monarch
begins to fly south in midsummer and autumn. This is a multigenerational cycle because most of the butterflies do not survive,
but they do lay eggs for the next generation.
Monarch butterflies east of the Rocky Mountains migrate to Mexico or Florida; those west
of the Rocky Mountains migrate to southern
California (Rosenblatt, 1998). The monarchs
seem to have a natural instinct that tells them
when to go and where to fly.

Linguistic
Logical-
Mathematical
Spatial

• Locate Canada, California, Mexico, Florida,
  Rocky Mountains, and Oyamel, Mexico on a
  map. Ask students to draw a map of the
  United States and plot the eastern and western migrations of the monarch butterfly. Begin the migration in the northern states and
  Canada. Point out that Oyamel, Mexico, is a
  stopping-off point for millions of butterflies.
  They rest in fir trees in the moist forests in
  central Mexico. They remain in a semidor-
  mant state during the winter months. When
  spring arrives, they wake up and begin to
  mate so they can lay eggs and continue the
  generational process before they die.

Logical-
Mathematical
Spatial

• Assist students in creating a monarch annual
  cycle that reflects their migration and indicates what happens in summer, fall, winter,
  and spring.

Bodily-
Kinesthetic
Spatial

• As a class, work together to create a butterfly
  garden in a window box. Plant flowers that
  have bright colors like yellow, orange, and
  red. Place fresh fruit, like watermelon and
  pineapple, in the garden. Place a small dish of
  fresh water for the butterflies to drink.

Linguistic
Logical-
Mathematical
Spatial

- Write information about butterflies and moths by using the letters of the words:

<u>B</u>eautiful   <u>M</u>etamorphosis
<u>U</u>nique   <u>O</u>riginal
<u>T</u>horax   <u>T</u>ransformation
<u>T</u>ransformation   <u>H</u>indwing
<u>E</u>xoskeleton   <u>S</u>hed
<u>R</u>emarkable
<u>F</u>orewing
<u>L</u>epidoptera
<u>Y</u>ellow

Assessments

- Students are to select two of the following methods for assessing this unit.
  - Raise both a butterfly and a moth in cardboard boxes or small cages with a plastic top or screen. Obtain fresh milkweed leaves (20 to 30 per insect) for a monarch butterfly. Find eggs and put them in the boxes. Wait for the eggs to hatch. Document the metamorphosis process daily. Keep a scientific log and graph a growth chart that measures the growth by length in comparison to the number of days in the different stages of metamorphosis. In a journal, write observations. Draw the different stages in the journal.
  - Explore the metamorphosis of tadpoles into frogs. How is their life cycle process different from butterflies and moths? How are they alike?
  - Create an autobiographical book written as if the students were the egg and share the stages of life of the butterfly, the moth, or both. Describe what occurs during the different stages. Illustrate the book. The story should be creative, but also should cite accurate content knowledge.
  - Write a song that teaches about the butterfly and the moth and exhibits in-depth content knowledge.
  - Write a play that covers information about butterflies and moths. Have a group of students perform the play.

Standards

The *Mathematics Content Standards* included in this unit are mathematical reasoning, computation skills, problem-solving skills, and the ability to communicate about quantities, logical relationships, and unknowns via symbols, graphs, and mathematical terms.

The *Science Content Standards* included in this unit focus on life sciences with an emphasis on sequential stages of life cycles, adaptations in physical structures or behavior that improve an organism's chance for survival, structure and function in living systems, and investigation and experimentation.

The *Language Arts Content Standards* included in this unit are in reading, writing, listening, and speaking. The writing standards focus on organization, revising and evaluating writing, writing autobiographies, and written and oral English language conventions. The reading areas addressed in this unit are decoding and word recognition, vocabulary and concept development, word analysis, and comprehension and analysis of text. Students are asked in this unit to listen carefully to the information provided and to share that information by speaking to a partner.

The *History/Social Science Content Standards* included in this unit are chronological and spatial thinking that require students to use map and global skills to determine location of specific places.

Unit 7

The Blending of Our Rainbow World

Objectives

- To develop respect for other cultures
- To understand and respect the unique differences in individuals
- To use writing to express feeling and to communicate expository information
- To demonstrate aesthetic, poetic writing
- To organize and deliver oral communications through storytelling

Content Areas Included in This Unit
Language Arts, History/Social Science, Mathematics, Science, and Art

Activities

Linguistic

- *Introduction*

- Read to the class "The Legend of the Dream Catcher."

  Long ago when the world was young, an old Lakota spiritual leader was on a high mountain and had a vision. In his vision, Iktomi, the great trickster and teacher of wisdom, appeared in the form of a spider. Iktomi spoke to him in a sacred language. As he spoke, Iktomi the spider picked up the elder's willow hoop, which had feathers, horsehair, beads, and offerings on it, and began to spin a web.

He spoke to the elder about the cycles of life: how we begin our lives as infants, move on through childhood, and into adulthood. Finally, we go to old age where we must be taken care of as infants again, completing the cycle. "But," Iktomi said as he continued to spin his web, "in each time of life there are may forces; some good and some bad. If you listen to the good forces, they will steer you in the right direction, but if you listen to the bad forces, they will steer you in the wrong direction and may hurt you. So these forces can help or can interfere with the harmony of Nature." While the spider spoke, he continued to weave his web.

When Iktomi finished speaking, he gave the leader the web and said, "The web is a

perfect circle with a hole in the center. Use the web to help your people reach their goals, making good use of their ideas, dreams; and visions. If you believe in the great spirit, the web will catch your good ideas and the bad ones will go through the hole." The elder passed on his vision to the people and now many Native Americans hang a dream catcher above their bed to sift their dreams and visions. The good is captured in the web of life and carried with the people, but the evil in their dreams is released through the hole in the center of the web and is no longer a part of their lives. It is said that the dream catcher holds the destiny of the future. (Excerpted from http:// www.dreamcatchers.org/ dcat16T.html.)

Linguistic
Interpersonal

• Ask students to discuss what this story means. Dialogue with a partner what the web of life means.

Spatial
Linguistic
Interpersonal

• Show a dream catcher to the class. Ask them to explain to a partner what they observe.

Linguistic

• Read about the dream catcher.

The dream catcher was made from a hoop of willow with a woven sinew. The Native Americans have been known to carry them in dances and special ceremonies. Many believe that individuals learn through their dreams and that dreams are visions that protect, guide, and assist individuals with their lives.

Dream catchers are usually hung above beds to protect the dreamer and assist in remembering the good dreams. Dream catchers can be made from metal or wooden hoops, deer hide, sinew, beads, and feathers. Sometimes they are given to babies when they are born, but can be given to individuals of all ages.

A dream catcher resembles a spider's web and is formed from one strand. It is a symbol of eternity and of the great circle of life. While a person dreams, good dreams are captured

Dream Catcher

Good dreams can pass on through,

Bad dreams are caught for you,

And disappear at morning light

When you awake without a fright.

and enter into the web of life. Bad dreams are said to be held in the webbing and disappear when the first rays of sun appear.

It is believed that by using a dream catcher, a person is able to sleep peacefully through the night and remember only the good dreams when they awaken. (Excerpted from http://nald.ca/province/ont/onlc/sample.htm.)

Linguistic
Interpersonal

• Ask four students to volunteer to each read a line of a poem about a dream catcher. Put the words on a transparency so all the class can see them.

Logical-
Mathematical
Interpersonal

- Ask students to divide into small groups to discuss what this poem means. What do dream catchers really do? Do they work? How?

Musical
Linguistic
Spatial

- Play the audio tape "Dream Catcher" by Ron Allen (Avalon Music, 1995). The music represents the cycles of life, death, and rebirth. Play "Spring Equinox" on the tape for the students. Tell them this music represents a great celebration of rebirth and renewal. Ask them to write or draw how they respond to this music and what they hear and see as they listen.

Linguistic

- The music "Dream Catcher" represents the medicine wheel of spring, summer, fall, and winter. Spring represents east and childhood, and is physical. Summer signifies south and adolescence, and is social. Fall represents west and parenthood, and is mental. Winter is located on the north side of the wheel and signifies old age and is spiritual.

Spatial

- Show to students a medicine wheel. Explain to them that it demonstrates the effort to seek and maintain balance and harmony in one's life.

Logical-
Mathematical
Interpersonal

- Point out the circle. Discuss as a group what a circle means. What are things that represent a circle in nature? (Be sure students discuss planets, sun, moon, and the Earth.) Ask why they are all in the shape of a circle.

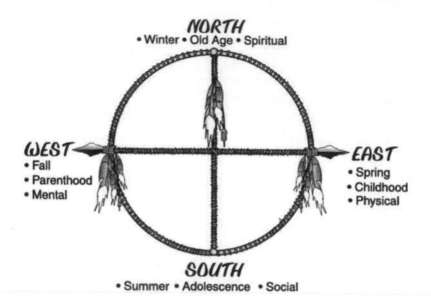

NORTH
• Winter • Old Age • Spiritual

WEST
• Fall
• Parenthood
• Mental

EAST
• Spring
• Childhood
• Physical

SOUTH
• Summer • Adolescence • Social

Logical- *Mathematical*	• Discuss the mathematical properties of a circle. What is the formula for circumference, radius, diameter, pi, and area of a circle?
Bodily- *Kinesthetic* *Interpersonal* *Logical-* *Mathematical*	• Divide into groups of 8 to 10 students. Act out what each of the formulas mean. Demonstrate to the other groups how to show what each of the formulas means.
Linguistic *Spatial* *Logical-* *Mathematical* *Interpersonal*	• Draw or write what pi, circumference, radius, diameter, and area of a circle mean. Create a problem that requires doing the mathematical computations. Ask other students to solve the problem. Check their answers.

Linguistic
Spatial
Intrapersonal

- Ask students to create their own medicine wheel that represents how they envision their circle of life. Share with them that many Native Americans believe the circle of life leads individuals back to where they came from, that the circle is complete and unending, that everything has a natural order, and that it is important to mend broken circles on Earth. Ask them what this means.

Linguistic
Spatial

- Introduce the concept of a circle of courage where the four elements are spirits of belonging, mastery, independence, and generosity. Ask students to place these four elements in their medicine wheel and decide where they fit and why.

Linguistic
Intrapersonal

- Ask students to write on paper the following five things:
  - A vision they have for their future
  - Three goals they can set for themselves
  - How they can make changes in their lives to more effectively reach these goals
  - What they believe are their greatest skills and talents
  - How they can best use their gifts and talents

Linguistic

- Read aloud *The Sunflower* (MacGregor, 1994). Share with the class that the author was only 12 years old when he wrote and illustrated this book. This story describes how a young Indian boy, who was called Dreamer, went in search of the seeds of the sunflower that would return sunlight to the Earth and save his people from starvation.

Linguistic *Spatial*	• Ask students to draw or write what they hear as the story is read aloud. Discuss the symbolism of the following:

The Sunflower	The Wind
Winter People	The Earth
Dreamer	Dreamer's Teardrops

Linguistic	• Look for descriptive words that enhance the story.
Logical- *Mathematical*	• What would the Earth be like if the sun did not shine? What would happen? Why? What is humankind's relationship to nature? Think of the sun, moon, Earth, mountains, desert, lakes, rivers, and ocean.
Linguistic *Spatial* *Intrapersonal*	• Ask students to select one of the elements of nature mentioned in the preceding activity and draw or write how that element relates to them personally.
Linguistic *Intrapersonal* *Spatial*	• Much of Native American culture and history has been passed to future generations through stories. Ask students to research their family's story and write about their heritage in a story format. They are to draw the most important parts of their story. Select a few students to tell their stories to the class.
Linguistic *Interpersonal* *Logical-* *Mathematical* *Bodily-* *Kinesthetic*	• Ask students to bring in a food from a different country or culture and be prepared to share how the food is used in that culture. For example, individuals might take an apple to treat a cold in Japan, an orange in the United States, and vegemite in Australia. Compare and contrast the foods. The students are to discuss their reactions to the different foods

when they tasted, smelled, and looked at them. How are different types of food a part of certain customs in various countries?

Linguistic

- Ask students to identify different customs that are unique to certain cultures. For example, bowing is a polite form of greeting in Japan, whereas, in the United States, it is customary to shake hands.

Linguistic
Logical-
Mathematical
Bodily-
Kinesthetic
Interpersonal
Intrapersonal

- Ask the students to stand and to respond to certain words as they are spoken by finding a group with which they believe they are similar. When they find the group, ask them to discuss with other students in that group how they are similar and how they are different. (This exercise is adapted from an exercise Dr. Carlos Cortes and I have taught together.) The sequence of the groups is as follows:
  - All males go to one side of the room and all females to the other side.
  - The groups are to gather based on the color of their eyes—brown eyes, blue eyes, and other colors.
  - The students are to find the group that represents the color of their hair—red hair, brown hair, black hair, blonde hair.
  - The students are to find the group that represents where they were born—Africa, Asia, Australia, Central America, Europe, North America, South America. Ask students to locate each of these continents on a map or a globe.
  - The students are to find the group they believe best represents their ethnic or cultural background—African American, Hispanic, white, Asian, other.

- The students are to find the group that processes in the dominant way they process based on the theory of multiple intelligences —linguistic, logical-mathematical, spatial, musical, bodily-kinesthetic, intrapersonal, interpersonal.

Intrapersonal

• The students can opt out of any of the exercises at any time.

Interpersonal
Linguistic

• When the activity is completed, have the students discuss how they felt during the exercises.

Linguistic
Logical-
Mathematical
Spatial
Musical
Bodily-
Kinesthetic
Intrapersonal
Interpersonal

• If it is possible to obtain permission from Walt Disney Company, show to the class the 5-minute clip from *Pocahontas* where Pocahontas sings "Colors of the Wind" to Captain John Smith. Then play the *Sing along Songs* version of "Colors of the Wind." Show them one right after another with no discussion. Then play the CD or audio cassette version of "Colors of the Wind" (Wonderland Music Company/Walt Disney Music Company, 1995). When the students have experienced all three, allow them to reflect on what they heard in each of the versions and which version they preferred and why. Discuss this with a partner and compare selections. Identify which intelligences were dominant in each of the versions.

Linguistic
Logical-
Mathematical

• Discuss as a class the following reflections:
  - Because we cannot see someone through new eyes, we may view individuals as ignorant savages. Why does this happen?
  - Who really owned the land? Captain John Smith, Pocahontas, or others? Why did they think they owned the land?

- What does the statement mean, "You think the only people who are people are the people who look and think like you"?
- What does the lyric mean, "We are all connected to each other in a circle that never ends"? Is this the circle of life that we studied?

Linguistic *Interpersonal*	• Read to the class the poem, "We and They" by Rudyard Kipling. Ask the students to discuss with a partner what this poem means.
Logical- *Mathematical* *Linguistic*	• Discuss with the class the importance of understanding the similarities and differences of others. It is important to learn how to build on the individual strengths everyone can contribute to society.
Linguistic *Spatial* *Intrapersonal* *Interpersonal*	• Share with students the book *A Rainbow at Night* (Hucko, 1996). Read one or two selections written and drawn by Navajo children. Ask students to write something about their own culture and then paint or draw to describe what they have written. Ask several students to share their work with the class.
Linguistic *Spatial*	• Discuss with students the different ways they process information. Review multiple intelligences with the students. Ask them how they can respect and appreciate the unique gifts, talents, and differences of others.
Linguistic *Spatial*	• Read *The Legend of the Indian Paintbrush* (De-Paola, 1988) to the class. Ask students to draw what they hear as the story is read. Why did Little Gopher change his name? Who is the circle of the people? What was his dream

vision? How was he able to appreciate his unique gifts and talents?

Linguistic
Intrapersonal

• Discuss with students that when they can identify and acknowledge each other's differences, the uniqueness of each individual, and the contributions only they can make.

Musical
Intrapersonal
Linguistic
Spatial

• To complete this unit, play the song, "The Power of the Dream" by Celine Dione, which was sung at the 1996 Olympics. Ask students to write or draw what they experience as they listen to the song. What is the theme or message of the song?

Linguistic   • Ask students to write a cinquain about the
Logical-   power of a dream, about the dream catcher,
Mathematical   or about appreciation of each other's cultures.
Musical   An example is given below.
Intrapersonal

Linguistic   • Ask students to read their cinquain to a part-
Interpersonal   ner. When they finish, they should turn to
                         each other and say, "You are a marvel. You
                         are unique. Thank you for being you."

Assessments

- The students are to select two to three of the works they
  have completed in this unit and place it in their portfolio or
  record of achievement.
- Students are to select two of the following measures of
  assessment:
  - Write a story that describes an individual from a different
    culture. Be creative, but compare and contrast the
    differences in that culture from your own culture.
  - Design a dream catcher. Write down instructions for
    making one and create it by following your instructions.
    Make something unique with the design that is symbolic.
    In a brochure, explain information about the dream catcher.
  - Write and illustrate a book that demonstrates the need to
    understand and respect the unique differences in
    individuals and cultures.
  - Write a song that discusses the similarities and differences
    between individuals and reflects the power we have to
    succeed.
  - Create a design that explains the cycle of life.

Standards

The *Mathematics Content Standards* included in this unit are
measurement and geometry, where students identify and describe
elements that compose common figures in the plane and common

objects in space, and mathematical reasoning, where students use skills and concepts to find solutions.

The *History/Social Science Content Standards* included in this unit are continuity and change, where students describe the American Indian nations in their local region long ago and in the recent past in terms of customs, religious beliefs, and folklore traditions. Place in time and space is covered when students compare and contrast the similarities and differences in everyday life in different times and places around the world, and describe human characteristics of familiar places and varied backgrounds of how American Indians and immigrant populations helped define American culture. The unit also includes activities that involve chronological and spatial thinking, historical research, and evidence, point of view, and historical interpretation.

The *Language Arts Content Standards* that are included in the unit are writing that focuses on compositions that represent analytical thought and demonstrate understanding of standard English, sentences and paragraphs that elaborate a central overall theme, and descriptive words that are used in writing compositions and poetry. The reading areas addressed in the unit are word analysis, vocabulary development, spelling, reading comprehension, and analysis of text.

The *Science Content Standards* are only touched on briefly with reference to the relationship of the Earth to the sun, moon, planets, and elements of nature and humankind's relationship to nature.

References

Ahrens, C. D. (1994). *An introduction to weather climate and the environment*. Belmont, CA: West/Wadsworth.

Allen, L. S., Richey, M. F., Chai, Y. M., & Gorski, R. A. (1991). Sex differences in the corpus callosum of the living human being. *The Journal of Neuroscience, 11*, 933–942.

Arizona State University. (1997). Available at URL:http://acept.la. asu.edu/pin/rdg/rainbow2.shtml

Armstrong, T. (1993). *7 kinds of smart*. New York: Penguin.

Armstrong, T. (1994). *Multiple intelligences in the classroom*. Alexandria, VA: Association for Supervision and Curriculum Development.

Arnosky, J. (1996). *Crinkleroots guide to knowing butterflies and moths*. New York: Simon and Schuster.

Baenninger, M., & Newcombe, N. C. (1989). The role of experience in spatial test performance: A meta-analysis. *Sex Roles, 20*, 327–344.

Baker, L. (1990). *Life in the rainforest*. New York: Scholastic.

Binet, A., & Simon, T. (1916). *The development of intelligence in children*. Baltimore, MD: Williams and Wilkins.

Bloom, B. S., Englehart, M. D., Furst, E. J., Hill, W. H., & Krathwohl, D. R. (1956). *Taxonomy of educational objectives: Handbook, cognitive domains*. New York: McKay.

Blythe, T., & Gardner, H. (1990). A school for all intelligence. *Educational Leadership*, April, 33–36.

Bolanos, P. J. (1990). Restructuring the curriculum. *Principal*, January, 13–14.

Bouton, D. A. (1997). *Operationalizing multiple intelligences theory with adolescent males*. Unpublished doctoral dissertation, Virginia Commonwealth University.

Boyer, C. B. (1959). *The rainbow from myth to mathematics*. New York: Yoseloff.

Bransford, J., Brown, A., & Cocking, R. (1999). *How people learn*. Washington, DC: National Academy Press.

Bruno, M. (1989). *Pocket pal*. Nashville, TN: International Paper Company.

Calaprice, A. (1996). *The quotable Einstein*. Princeton, NJ: Princeton University Press.

Carle, E. (1987). *The very hungry caterpillar*. New York: Pilomel Books.

Ceci, S. J. (1990). *On intelligence... more or less a biological treatise on intellectual development*. Englewood Cliffs, NJ: Prentice Hall.

Charlesworth, L. (1997). *Colors of the rainforest*. New York: Scholastic.

Cherry, L. (1990). *Great kapok tree: A tale of the Amazon rainforest*. New York: Harcourt Brace.

Crist, M. (1990). *Electrophysiological correlates of drawing in a very young child*. Unpublished doctoral dissertation, Columbia University Teachers College.

Crozat, F. (1993). *I am a little panda*. New York: Barron.

Cunningham, A. (1993). *Rainforests wildlife*. London: Usborne.

Cwiklik, R. (1987). *Albert Einstein and the theory of relativity*. New York: Barron.

De Paola, T. (1988). *The legend of the indian paintbrush*. New York: Putnam.

Dewey, J. (1902). *The child and the curriculum*. Chicago: University of Chicago Press.

Diamond, M. (1988). *Enriching heredity: The impact of the environment on the brain*. New York: Free Press.

Feeney, K. (1997). *Pandas for kids*. Minocqua, WI: Northword Press.

Feuerstein, R. (1981). Cognitive modifiability in adolescence: Cognitive structure and the effects of intervention. *The Journal of Special Education, 15*, 269–286.

Fullan, M. G. (1991). *The new meaning of educational change* (2nd ed.). New York: Teachers College Press.

Gardner, H. (1983). *Frames of mind: The theory of multiple intelligences*. New York: Basic.

Gardner, H., & Hatch, T. C. (1989). Multiple intelligences goes to school—Educational implications of the theory of multiple intelligences. *Educational Researchers, 18* (8), 4–9.

Gardner, H. (1990). *The Churchill Forum*, 2–7.

Gardner, H. (1991). *The unschooled mind: How children think and how schools should teach*. New York: Basic Books.

Gardner, H. (1993). *Multiple intelligences: The theory in practice*. New York: Basic Books.

Gardner, H. (1996). *Are there additional intelligences? The case for naturalist, spiritual and existential intelligences*. Unpublished manuscript.

Gardner, H. (1997). Multiple intelligences as a partner in school improvement. *Educational Leadership, 55*, 20–21.

Garland, T. H. (1987). *Fascinating Fibonacci mystery and magic in numbers*. Palo Alto, CA: Dale Seymour Publications.

Goleman, D. (1995). *Emotional intelligence.* New York: Bantam.

Green, J. (1995). *The green book.* Nashville, TN: Professional Desk References, Inc.

Halpern, D. (1992). *Sex differences in cognitive abilities,* Hillsdale, NJ: Erlbaum.

Halpern, D. F., & Crothers, M. (1997). *The sexual orientation: Biological understanding.* Westport, CT: Praeger.

Harris, J. R. (1995). Where is the child's environment? A group socialization theory of development. *Psychological Review, 102,* 458–489.

Hart, L. (1983). *Human brain and human learning.* Kent, WA: Books for Education.

Hinshaw, D. (1997). *Flashy fantastic rainforest frogs.* New York: Walker and Company.

Hoerr, T. R. (1994). How the New York City School applies the multiple intelligences. *Educational Leadership, 52,* 24–34.

Hucko, B. (1996). *A rainbow at night.* San Francisco: Chronicle Books.

Innocenti, G. M. (1994). Some new trends in the study of the research of corpus callosum. *Behavioral and Brain Research, 64,* 1–8.

Jancke, L., & Steinmetz, H. (1994). Interhemispheric-transfer time and corpus callosum size. *Neuroreport, 5,* 2385–2388.

Jensen, E. (1995). *The learning brain.* San Diego, CA: Turning Point Publishing.

Julivert, A. (1991). *Butterflies and moths.* New York: Barron's.

Kalman, B., & Everts, T. (1994). *Bugs and other insects.* New York: Crabtree.

Kornhaber, M. L. (1997). *Seeking strengths: equitable identification for gifted education and the theory of multiple intelligences.* Unpublished doctoral dissertation, Harvard University.

Lawrence Hall of Science. (1989). *Color analyzer.* Berkeley, CA: Regents of the University of California.

Le Doux, J. E. (1994). Emotion, memory and brain. *Scientific American, 270* (6), 50–57.

Le Doux, J. E. (1996). *The emotional brain: The mysterious underpinnings of emotional life.* New York: Simon and Schuster.

Legg, G. (1997). *Creepy critters.* New York: Smithmark Publishers.

Leinhardt, G. (1988). Getting to know: Tracing students' mathematical knowledge from intuition to competence. *Educational Psychologist, 23,* 119–144.

Lynds, B. (1997). *About rainbows.* Available at http://www.unidata.ucar.edu.staff/blynds/mbw.html.

MacGregor, M. (1994). *The sunflower.* Kansas City, MO: Landmark Editions.

Macmillan/McGraw. (1993). *Science turns minds on.* New York: Macmillan/McGraw-Hill School Division.

Martin, B. (1989). *Chicka, chicka, boom, boom.* New York: Little Simon.

Martin, B. (1995). *Brown bear, brown bear, what do you see?* New York: Holt.

Mathers, D. (1992). *You and your brain.* London: Troll Associates.

National Commission on Teaching and America's Future (1996). *What matters most: Teaching for America's future.* New York: National Commission on Teaching and America's Future (NCTAF).

National Institutes of Health. (1996). Education: The human cerebral cortex. *Journal of NIH Research, 8.*

Nayer, J. (1993). *The rainforest.* Columbus, OH: Modern Curriculum Press.

Nefsky, P. (1997). *The effectiveness of authentic assessment and multiple intelligences theory with an individual with developmental disabilities.* Unpublished masters thesis, California State University, Long Beach.

Offutt, M. (1990). *Chemistry songbag.* Batavia, IL: Flinn Scientific.

O'Neill, M. (1961). *Hailstones and halibut bones.* New York: Doubleday.

Parker, J. (1997). *Rainforest.* New York: Ladybird.

Petty, K. (1992). *Pandas.* New York: Barron's.

Pfister, M. (1992). *The rainbow fish.* New York: North–South Books.

Piaget, J. (1951). *Play, dreams and imitation in childhood.* New York: W. W. Norton.

Piaget, J. (1972). *The psychology of intelligence.* Norwood, NJ: Littlefield Adams.

Reed, T. E., & Jensen, A. R. (1993). Choice reaction time and visual pathway conduction velocity both correlate with intelligence. Implications for information processing. *Intelligence, 17,* 199–203.

Roesch, D. E. (1997). *An ethnographic qualitative study of the perspectives of English teachers on the use of multiple intelligences theory in the high school classroom.* Unpublished masters thesis, St. Louis University.

Rosenblatt, L. (1998). *Monarch magic.* Charlotte, VT: Williamson Publishing Company.

Rossbach, S., & Yun, L. (1994). *Living color*. New York: Kodansha.

San Diego Zoo. (1995). *Zoobooks—Butterflies*. San Diego: Wildlife Education.

Seuss, Dr. (1996). *My many colored days*. New York: Random House.

Shaywitz, B. A., Shaywitz, S. E., Pugh, K. R., Constable, R. T., Skullarski, P., Fulbright, R. K., Bronen, R. A., Fletcher, J. M., Shankweller, D. P., Katz, L., & Gore, J. C. (1995). Sex differences in the functional organization of the brain for language. *Nature, 373*, 607–609.

Shlain, L. (1991). *Art and physics—Parallel visions in space, time and light*. New York: Morrow.

Simon, S. (1997). *The brain—Our nervous system*. New York: Morrow.

Smagorinsky, P. (1991). Multiple intelligences. Multiple means of composing: an alternative way of thinking about learning. *NASSP Bulletin, 80*, 18–24.

Spearman, C. (1927). *The abilities of man: Their nature and measurement*. New York: McMillan.

State of California State Board of Education. (1997a). *The California language arts content standards* (pre-publication version). Sacramento: State Board of Education.

State of California State Board of Education. (1997b). *The California mathematics academic content standards* (pre-publication version). Sacramento: State Board of Education.

State of California State Board of Education. (1998a). *History / social science content standards grade K–12* (pre-publication version). Sacramento: State Board of Education.

State of California State Board of Education. (1998b). *Science content standards grade K–12* (pre-publication version). Sacramento: State Board of Education.

Steinmetz, H. J., Staiger, J. F., Schluag, G., Huang, Y., & Jancke, L. (1995). Corpus callosum and brain volume in women and men. *Neuroreport, 6*, 1002–1004.

Sternberg, R. J. (1985). *Beyond IQ: A triarchic theory of human intelligence*. New York. Cambridge University Press.

Sternberg, R. J. (1988). *The nature of creativity*. New York: Cambridge University Press.

Stimson, J. (1993). *Big panda, little panda*. New York: Barron's.

Stone, B., & Eckstein, A. (1983). *Preparing art for printing*. New York: Van Nostrand Reinhold.

Sylwester, R. (1995). *A celebration of neurons*. Alexandria, VA: Association for Supervision and Curriculum Development.

Teele, S. (1992). *Teele inventory of multiple intelligences*. Redlands, CA: Citrograph Printing.

Teele, S. (1994). *The multiple intelligences school: A place for all students to succeed*. Redlands, CA: Citrograph Printing.

Treays, R. (1995). *Understanding your brain*. London: Usborne.

Ungerleider, L. G. (1995). Functional brain imaging studies of cortical mechanisms for memory. *Science, 270,* 769–775.

University of Illinois. (1997). Available at http://covis.atmos.uluc. edu/ guide/ optics/ rainbows/ html/rain.formation.html.

U.S. Department of Education. (1996). *Third international mathematics and science study*. Washington, DC: U.S. Department of Education.

Vogel, G. (1996). School achievement: Asia and Europe top in world, both reasons are hard to find. *Science, 274,* 1296.

Vygotsky, L. S. (1978). *Mind in society. The development of higher psychological processes*. Cambridge, MA: Harvard University Press.

Woolf, L. (1997). *It's a colorful life*. San Diego: General Atomics Science Education Foundation.

Woolf, L. (1999). Confusing color concepts clarified. *The Physics Teacher, 37* (4), 204–206.

Yolen, J. (1993). *Welcome to the green house*. New York: Paper Star Book.